Viking Tales and Sagas

The Captivating Tale of Ragnar Lothbrok, Ivar the Boneless, Lagertha, and More as well as Other Legendary Stories of Vikings in Their Historical Context

© Copyright 2020

All Rights Reserved. No part of this book may be reproduced in any form without permission in writing from the author. Reviewers may quote brief passages in reviews.

Disclaimer: No part of this publication may be reproduced or transmitted in any form or by any means, mechanical or electronic, including photocopying or recording, or by any information storage and retrieval system, or transmitted by email without permission in writing from the publisher.

While all attempts have been made to verify the information provided in this publication, neither the author nor the publisher assumes any responsibility for errors, omissions or contrary interpretations of the subject matter herein.

This book is for entertainment purposes only. The views expressed are those of the author alone, and should not be taken as expert instruction or commands. The reader is responsible for his or her own actions.

Adherence to all applicable laws and regulations, including international, federal, state and local laws governing professional licensing, business practices, advertising and all other aspects of doing business in the US, Canada, UK or any other jurisdiction is the sole responsibility of the purchaser or reader.

Neither the author nor the publisher assumes any responsibility or liability whatsoever on the behalf of the purchaser or reader of these materials. Any perceived slight of any individual or organization is purely unintentional.

Free Bonus from Captivating History (Available for a Limited time)

Hi History Lovers!

Now you have a chance to join our exclusive history list so you can get your first history ebook for free as well as discounts and a potential to get more history books for free! Simply visit the link below to join.

Captivatinghistory.com/ebook

Also, make sure to follow us on Facebook, Twitter and Youtube by searching for Captivating History.

Contents

PART 1: VIKING SAGAS 1
THE CAPTIVATING TALE OF RAGNAR LOTHBROK, IVAR THE BONELESS, LAGERTHA, AND MORE, IN THEIR HISTORICAL CONTEXT 1
INTRODUCTION: THE VIKING AGE 2
PART I: THE WORLD OF RAGNAR LOTHBROK 5
NOTES TO THE WORLD OF RAGNAR LOTHBROK 31
PART II: THE SAGA OF RAGNAR LOTHBROK AND HIS SONS 36
NOTES TO THE SAGA OF RAGNAR LOTHBROK AND HIS SONS 65
PART III: REPRESENTATIONS OF NORSE MYTHS AND HISTORY IN MODERN MEDIA 71
NOTES TO "DRAGONS IN TOLKIEN'S MIDDLE-EARTH" 79
THE CLASH OF HISTORY AND DRAMA IN THE HISTORY CHANNEL TELEVISION SERIES *VIKINGS* 86
NOTES TO "THE CLASH OF HISTORY AND DRAMA IN THE HISTORY CHANNEL TELEVISION SERIES *VIKINGS*" 95
APPENDIX: THE TALE OF SIGURD AND BRYNHILD 103
PART 2: TALES FROM THE VIKING AGE 111
CAPTIVATING LEGENDARY AND HISTORICAL SAGAS 111
INTRODUCTION 112
THE SAGA OF KING HEIDREK THE WISE 115
SELECTIONS FROM THE SAGA OF ÖRVAR-ODDR 152

THE VOYAGES TO VINLAND 171
REFERENCES 201

Part 1: Viking Sagas

The Captivating Tale of Ragnar Lothbrok, Ivar the Boneless, Lagertha, and More, in Their Historical Context

Introduction: The Viking Age

The period between the end of the eighth century CE and the middle of the eleventh is often called the "Viking Age" because this is the period in which Scandinavian people expanded their contacts with the outside world through trade, raiding, exploration, and colonization. This expansion was driven by improvements in shipbuilding technology combined with a culture that valued personal reputation, courage, and martial skill as essential components of one's character, at least for the male portion of the population.

Archaeological evidence can tell us much about how early Scandinavian people lived and died, but it can only take us so far. It is not until the Viking Age that we begin to have enough written evidence to reconstruct aspects of early Scandinavian history and culture. Writing other than runes, which were used for magical and religious purposes, for monuments, or for identifying possessions, was unknown in Scandinavia until the advent of Christianity, which began with Anglo-Saxon missionary efforts in the early eighth century and had taken hold throughout Scandinavia by the twelfth century. The earliest Scandinavian documents, therefore, date from the twelfth century, the period during which Christianity became widespread.

The limited contacts between Scandinavia and more southerly countries all changed in the late eighth century, and the shift is usually dated to the sudden increase in large-scale Viking raids on important religious and political centers, such as the monasteries of Lindisfarne in England in 793 and Iona in Scotland in 795. Incursions into Frankish territory, part of which encompassed areas in what are now France, Germany, and the Low Countries, followed in 799. Further attacks on cities in England and the Frankish Empire increased throughout the ninth century, including the sack of Paris in 845 by a Viking named Ragnar (who may or may not have been the Lothbrok of the saga) and the invasion of England by the so-called "Great Army" in 879.

Most often we know of these attacks not from the perspective of the Vikings themselves but rather from the point of view of their victims and the later medieval historians who recorded what they knew or had been able to learn of these events. Medieval chronicles, usually compiled by clergy in the Frankish Empire or in England, are important primary sources for the activities of Vikings at this time, and it is this view of Vikings as intrepid explorers and vicious plunderers that is at the core of modern popular conceptions about medieval Scandinavian culture.

However, the Viking Age was about much more than longships full of fierce warriors sailing across the seas and down rivers in order to pillage whatever and slay whomever they came across. Medieval Scandinavians also led complex lives that revolved around agriculture, artisanal crafts, and trade, none of which is as exciting to the imagination as a warrior's raid but which stood at the vital economic center of medieval Scandinavian life.

One important product of medieval Scandinavian culture is the corpus of sagas and poetry that first began to be recorded in writing in the twelfth century, although much of that corpus was composed significantly earlier and handed down through oral tradition. The *Saga of Ragnar Lothbrok* is one of these products, combining what may be a grain or two of historical fact with some fairy-tale episodes, connections to other aspects of Norse mythology, and a good helping of Viking derring-do.

This volume presents a version of Ragnar's saga compiled from different modern sources, along with information providing additional historical and documentary context, followed by a discussion of some aspects of modern appropriations and representations of ancient Norse culture. The first section of the book provides historical context for Ragnar's saga through an exploration of daily life in ninth-century Scandinavia and of contemporary Viking culture and history. The text of the saga itself forms the second part of the book, along with notes giving further information about how this version of the saga is presented and about elements within the story that might not be familiar to modern readers. The third section of the book deals with representations of ancient Norse cultures in modern popular media. Because this last topic is too large and too complex to be thoroughly explored in this current volume, I will focus on two areas: dragons in the writings of J. R. R. Tolkien and the conflicts between drama and history in the recent television miniseries, *Vikings*, which itself is based, in part, on the *Saga of Ragnar Lothbrok* and the *Tale of Ragnar's Sons*. And because the *Saga of Ragnar Lothbrok* has important connections to another Icelandic saga, the *Saga of the Volsungs*, a synopsis of *Volsungs* is provided in an appendix.

The Viking Age is a historical period rich with art, poetry, literature, trade, exploration, and battles. The *Saga of Ragnar Lothbrok* is a product of that time and presents to us a story of Vikings not only as they actually may have been, at least in part, but also as they wished to be seen and remembered by later generations. And we still do remember them, over a thousand years after they sailed in search of plunder, trade, and new lands.

Part I: The World of Ragnar Lothbrok

Life in Medieval Scandinavia

Farms and Dwellings

While the modern imagination is full of images of helmeted Vikings jumping out of longships brandishing swords, actual medieval Scandinavian life was rather more prosaic for the majority of the population. Agriculture, animal husbandry, and exploitation of wild food sources such as fish, game, and berries were vital to survival and were widely practiced throughout Scandinavian lands, with certain variations depending upon local climates. Medieval Scandinavians also were artisans who worked with metal, wood, and leather, and while Viking merchants mostly traded fairly close to home, Scandinavian trade routes, in fact, extended as far south as the Middle East and as far east as the Dnieper River, with further connections to the ancient Silk Road via trading posts and cities to the east and south of Viking territories.

In the parts of Scandinavia that were warm and fertile enough for agriculture, farmers grew crops such as barley and rye, pulses, cabbage, and hops. In addition, hemp for ropemaking and flax to spin and weave into linen cloth were also important agricultural products.ⁱ Cows and goats were kept for their milk, and sheep for their wool and meat. Pigs were raised for their meat, and poultry for their feathers, down, and eggs.ⁱⁱ The diet provided by farm produce was supplemented by fishing, hunting, and gathering wild foods such as berries, nuts, and herbs.ⁱⁱⁱ

Whether situated on a lonely farmstead or gathered into a village or town, the typical Viking dwelling was a longhouse with two or more sections. One end functioned as a byre for the domestic livestock, where their body heat helped to keep the house warm during the long, frigid Scandinavian winters. At the other end of the house was the space used for eating, sleeping, and tasks that often needed to be done indoors, such as spinning and weaving. Chieftains might have additional rooms, including one section that was used as the ceremonial hall in which they entertained guests and the warriors who fought for them.ⁱᵛ These great halls were also the places in which skalds recited their poetry in praise of the chieftain and where feasts in connection with religious sacrifices took place.ᵛ

Lowly farmhouses, the proud halls of the chieftains, and every sort of dwelling in between had a narrow firepit running down the length of the portions of the building used by the humans who lived there. The fire provided light, warmth, and heat to cook with, but it also created smoke that was not guided to the outside by a chimney; the sole escape for smoke was a small hole in the roof.ᵛⁱ

Towns, such as the important market center of Hedeby on the Jutland Peninsula, also might have workshops and warehouses in addition to dwellings. Further, archaeological evidence from Hedeby shows efforts at civil engineering in the form of wood-paved streets and wooden linings for the wells and the stream that ran through the town, presumably to keep the streets from churning into mud and to help keep the water supply as clean as possible.ᵛⁱⁱ It's probably fair to say that Hedeby was not the only community to engage in projects like these, which were aimed at improving the quality of life for the residents, but one wonders whether that sort of effort was also made by communities outside the larger and more prosperous towns.

Families and Gender Roles

The basic Viking family unit was what we call the nuclear family: a husband, a wife, and their children. However, many families fit into a larger household unit, which could include servants or slaves or both in addition to the basic family unit. Households also occasionally encompassed two or more nuclear families—plus servants or slaves, if any—living together and working the same land.[viii]

Gender roles in Viking society were strongly circumscribed. Men dealt with the things outside the house, while women dealt with the things inside. In practical terms, this meant that women managed the household, cared for the children, and were responsible for tasks such as spinning and weaving, sewing clothing, baking bread, cooking or preserving food, and brewing beer. Women were also responsible for collecting milk and making cheese and butter.

Men worked the land and went hunting or fishing, and they were also involved in judicial proceedings and other governing work, which women were forbidden to undertake.[ix] In areas where agriculture was difficult or impossible because of climactic conditions, men's work shifted to animal husbandry, hunting of marine mammals and other animals, and fishing, or some combination thereof.[x] Men also were the ones who fought and went on raids, but those who had families and farms to tend usually stayed home; the fierce, plundering Vikings with which modern people are familiar usually were younger, unmarried males who had little or no land of their own and who joined raiding parties in an attempt to bolster fortunes that were unlikely to be improved through the inheritance of family wealth.[xi]

That said, there is some evidence for the adventuresome nature of Viking women, some of whom fought alongside men and others of whom embarked on dangerous journeys, either on their own behalf or with male relatives. Much of the evidence for the existence and deeds of these women is found in the Icelandic sagas, including the *Saga of Ragnar Lothbrok*, in which one female warrior, Lagertha, plays an important role. A different version of Lagertha's story also appears alongside tales about other women warriors in the *Gesta Danorum* ("Deeds of the Danes"), a monumental history of Denmark written in the twelfth century by Danish historian Saxo Grammaticus.[xii]

While it is difficult to separate fact from fiction in the sagas and even in Saxo's carefully written history, physical evidence for Viking women as fighters is rather more reliable: an archeological study performed in 2017 confirmed that a Viking warrior who was buried at Birka in Sweden was indeed female.[xiii] In addition to the woman's skeleton, the authors of the paper report that the grave held "a sword, an axe, a spear, armour-piercing arrows, a battle knife, two shields, and two horses, one mare and one stallion; thus, the complete equipment of a professional warrior."[xiv] An examination of the skeleton's proportions and other attributes strongly suggested that the buried person was a woman, and later DNA testing confirmed female gender.[xv]

We don't know the name of the female warrior from Birka, but one adventurous woman in the saga literature who apparently was a real historical figure was Aud the Deep-Minded, the wife of the Viking king of Dublin, who lived in the ninth century. When Aud's husband was killed in battle, she packed up her entire household and moved everyone and everything to Iceland, where her brothers were already living.[xvi] Another historical figure is Freydis Eiriksdottir. Freydis was the sister of Leif Eiriksson (also commonly spelled as Erikson), the Viking who sailed to what is now Newfoundland in Canada in the eleventh century. The *Greenland Saga* tells the story of Freydis' organization of an expedition to Newfoundland on her own behalf sometime after her brother had constructed a small settlement there. This saga paints Freydis as a strong, ruthless, and conniving leader who is not above murdering those who stand in her way.[xvii]

Although some women did remain single and made their living by hiring themselves out for work, most women married.[xviii] Author Kirsten Wolf points out that before the advent of Christianity, marriage in Viking society was primarily a business arrangement between the man and the woman, and marrying for love seems to have been unknown.[xix] Negotiations for marriage were carried out between the woman's father and her suitor or her suitor's family, and she had little to no choice in the matter. However, women were able to seek divorce of their own accord and had a right to take their dowry (money paid by the woman's father to her spouse's family upon marriage) and personal property with them when they left the marriage. The woman also had the right to get the bride price (money paid to her father by the groom's family) if it turned out her husband was at fault for the dissolution of the marriage.[xx] As Wolf notes, Christianity radically changed attitudes toward marriage and divorce by conceptualizing marriage as a sacrament between the spouses that was intended to last until one or both of the partners died rather than a business deal that could be dissolved at will should it become unsatisfactory to one or both of the partners.[xxi]

For men, women, and children alike, life in medieval Scandinavia was difficult and full of hard work. Only those with higher social status might expect to escape at least some of the physical labor that most members of society had to do in order to provide for themselves and their families. Rudimentary medical care, chronic malnutrition, and a complete lack of vaccinations of any kind meant that disease was both distressingly common and often fatal and that lifespans were relatively short.[xxii] To reach one's sixtieth birthday was to achieve an advanced age, according to Anders Winroth.[xxiii]

The evidence for Winroth's conclusions comes from the examination of skeletons from Viking-era graves. Adult height is dependent on nutrition in childhood and, as Winroth reports, Viking adults were often fairly short by modern Western standards. Examinations of Danish Viking skeletons shows that women on average were only slightly over five feet tall (158 centimeters on average) and men were only about six inches or so taller (171 centimeters on average). Further, many of the skeletons show evidence of disease, iron deficiency, and broken bones.[xxiv] However, author Neil Oliver presents a rosier picture, stating that the average male height was about five feet eight inches (about 173 centimeters) and the average female height about five feet three inches (about 160 centimeters) and that teeth examined from Viking burials "suggests many people enjoyed a reasonable diet."[xxv] That said, whether one accepts Winroth's or Oliver's data as more representative of the health of medieval Scandinavians, to be a Viking one had to be tough, not just in terms of warfare but in terms of mere survival in living conditions that many modern people would consider difficult at best and appalling at worst.

Longships

At the end of the eighth century, Scandinavians expanded their interactions with the outside world. Sometimes these interactions came in the form of Viking raids, but more often they came in the form of trade relationships or colonization of new lands. These expansions had far-reaching effects, so much so that author Anders Winroth observes that the "overall impact of Scandinavian endeavors was, unexpectedly, to stimulate the economy of Western Europe," which had collapsed in the wake of the fall of Rome and was still struggling to recover three hundred years later.[xxvi]

The piece of technology that gave the Vikings an advantage in these undertakings was the longship. Living as they did in areas with long coastlines and relatively short journeys to the sea from most inland locations, the ancient Scandinavians were quick to develop boatmaking technologies. Petroglyphs from the Bronze Age indicate that Scandinavians had already been seafaring peoples for over two thousand years before the Viking Age began.[xxvii]

The longships sailed by the Vikings were clinker-built, meaning that they were constructed of overlapping planks riveted together and then coated with a sealant, usually tar or oil made from seal blubber, to keep them from rotting.[xxviii] Viking shipwrights also caulked the places where the planks overlapped with animal hair in order to make the ships watertight.[xxix]

Today, we tend to have an image of Viking ships as having one square sail and many oars, but that was a later development; earlier ships had neither mast nor sail and were instead propelled by oars alone.[xxx] On inland journeys along rivers, the ships might also be unloaded, and both ship and cargo would be carried from one point to another along stretches of the river that were unnavigable.[xxxi]

Although the basic pattern of all Viking ships was the same, they could be adjusted in length and beam in order to serve their intended purpose and in order to be able to function in the waters where they would be used. Wider ships might be used for trade because they could carry more cargo, and lighter, narrower ships might be used on rivers. But whatever their purpose, for raiding, trading, or exploration, longships were the most important piece of Viking technology and were the tools that connected medieval Scandinavians to the rest of the world.

The Vikings Abroad

Vikings as Traders

Vikings of course traded with one another within their own territories, but Viking trade routes also ran throughout Western and Central Europe, extending into the Arab Caliphate on the Iberian Peninsula and in the Middle East, Byzantium, and eastward into what are now Ukraine, Belarus, and Russia. These trade routes ran along the coastlines of Europe; through the Mediterranean, Caspian, and Black Seas; and along navigable rivers such as the Rhine, the Seine, the Dnieper, and the Volga. The easternmost portions of these trade routes gave the Vikings access to goods from the Far East and Southeast Asia, which traveled along the ancient Silk Road.[xxxii]

Goods exported from Scandinavia included amber, timber, walrus ivory, and honey.[xxxiii] Iron ore taken from bogs was in high demand outside Viking lands, as were furs, schist to turn into whetstones, and soapstone, which was shaped into vessels for cooking and eating.[xxxiv] Vikings, in turn, imported silk, spices, and jewelry from the East, while wine, glass, pottery, and weapons came from Western and Central Europe.[xxxv] The slave trade also was quite active at this time, with slaves being both imported and exported by Viking traders.[xxxvi]

One of the imports most valued by Vikings was silver. This often came into Scandinavia in the form of Arab coins called dirhams. Hoard after hoard containing hundreds of dirhams has been excavated in places such as Germany and Sweden. These hoards are important not only because they show Western European peoples in active trade with Arab countries but also because the coins are dated and therefore can give us an idea of when this trade was active.[xxxvii] Author Richard Hall reports that coins from Viking hoards indicate that "the eastern trade had started by the 780s, increased in the 860s-880s and grew dramatically to a peak in the 940s-950s. Thereafter decline set in as the central Asian silver mines were depleted."[xxxviii] Of course the increase in numbers of coins also tracks with the increase in Viking trade outside of Scandinavia, as well as with the increase in Viking raids.

The Vikings did not use these or any other coins as currency, however. Both Arab coins and gold and silver Christian sacred objects raided from church treasuries were often melted down and the metal exchanged for goods or services by weight. We know that the Vikings did not see dirhams and other foreign coinage as currency but rather as a source of raw metal because Viking hoards often contain both fragmentary and complete coins.[xxxix]

The expansion of Viking trade routes did more than stimulate the economy, provide livelihoods for producers of goods, and give Scandinavians access to exotic luxury items. The growth in trade was also a stimulus for the growth of towns, which could function as manufacturing, collection, and distribution hubs much more efficiently than the small groupings of farmsteads that had been the most common type of community before the eighth century.[xl]

We have already discussed some of the characteristics of the town of Hedeby in Jutland, which was one of the more important centers of trade in medieval Scandinavia. Places like Hedeby were permanent settlements that, in addition to dwellings, had multiple jetties for docking boats and workshops and warehouses for creating and storing goods. In addition to such towns, there were also smaller market centers that might exist only at certain times of the year, where traders would gather to buy, sell, and exchange their goods.[xli]

Kaupang in Norway was one such center. Kaupang may originally have been a village, but it appears to have become simply a market center by about 850.[xlii] Richard Hall reports that bead-making was one of the crafts pursued in Kaupang, and he also states that materials for making casted items such as brooches and materials for making jewelry have been found there.[xliii] Kaupang also has been a rich source of evidence for the kinds of things that were being imported into Viking lands from other places. According to Hall, these included

drinking glasses, pottery jugs and lava quernstones from the Frankish Rhineland, ... an Anglo-Saxon penny, ... Slavonic and Jutlandic pottery, and ... beads ... that may have come from places as widespread as Ireland, Ribe, Byzantium, the Black Sea/Caspian Sea region, and the Near and Middle East.[xliv]

While medieval Scandinavia certainly wasn't a cosmopolitan place, it wasn't isolated either. Vikings were busy collecting and making items to trade, and their trading practices connected them to places and peoples throughout Europe, Asia, and the Middle East. Just as with the practices of agriculture, hunting, and fishing, making crafts and trading were the occupations of a significant portion of the population, a much greater portion than was engaged in the raids that we so often associate with Viking culture.

Viking Raids

The first recorded Viking raid was on Portland in England in 789. The next reported raid, on the wealthy Northumbrian island monastery of Lindisfarne in 793, was even more violent than the one on Portland had been. Medieval English annals such as the *Anglo-Saxon Chronicle* record the terror and shock engendered by the Lindisfarne raid, wherein many of the monks were killed, others taken as slaves, and the monastery's treasury emptied of its gold, silver, silk vestments, and other valuables.[xlv] The sack of Lindisfarne was followed in 795 by another monastery raid, this time on Iona in the Inner Hebrides off the Scottish coast.[xlvi] With these three raids, the Viking Age is considered to have begun in earnest.

England was not the only target of Viking raids. The Frankish Empire also promised rich takings, and by the middle of the ninth century, Vikings had made several incursions into Frankish territory in addition to continuing their attacks on English soil. In 845, Vikings sailed down the Seine and attacked Paris. This raid was led by a man apparently named Ragnar, who may or may not have been the Lothbrok of the saga.[xlvii] (Ragnar's identity will be explored in more detail in a later chapter.) A further expansion of the territories considered ripe for plundering happened in 859, when Björn Ironsides, who likely was an actual historical personage and was said to be Ragnar's son, raided Spain. Björn then went on to raid Luni on Italy's Ligurian coast the following year.[xlviii]

Thirst for riches and a desire to prove oneself in battle were certainly part of the impetus for Viking men to take ship and sail across the sea to loot cities and towns, but this is only a very small part of the picture. Various cultural, social, and political factors also came into play, making ninth-century Scandinavia a launching pad primed for piratical attacks on other countries. One of these certainly was the Viking warrior culture, which greatly prized and rewarded courage and martial skill. However, it was the political structure in the earlier part of the Viking Age that brought these warriors together and created a framework in which they could prosper in their raiding activities.

Prior to the tenth century, the basic political unit in much of Scandinavia was the chiefdom, which could be passed from father to son, but succession to chieftainship in fact was much more fluid. Viking law and tradition allowed inheritance from both the mother's and the father's side, and as author John Haywood observes, "any man possessed of royal blood ... was eligible for kingship. Illegitimacy was no bar."[xlix]

Although a distinguished line of descent certainly was considered meritorious when putting oneself forward as a candidate for chieftainship, one's lineage was by no means the only consideration; many other factors contributed to whether a man might attain chieftainship, and these factors also determined whether and for how long he would be able to retain that position. The chieftain was accepted as a leader, but the hierarchical relationship stopped there. To the warriors at his command, the chieftain was first among equals, not superior to them. Anders Winroth states that Viking warriors "were not simple mercenaries fighting for pay; they were independent-minded and proud warriors who would fight alongside those they were bound to in honorable relations of friendship."[l]

To keep faith with his warriors, the chieftain was expected to be generous in the distribution of booty and other gifts, as well as in holding feasts and drinkings to which the warriors would be invited and at which the skalds, or poets, would perform songs and poems praising the exploits of the chieftain and his warriors.[li] As Winroth reports, gifts from the chieftain to his warriors were not simply payment for services rendered but rather the discharge of one side of a mutual obligation, the other side of which was the warrior's military service at the chieftain's command.[lii]

The size of Viking raiding parties no doubt varied depending on the number and size of ships and the number of armed men available. Neil Oliver estimates that one type of longship, the *drakkar* or "dragon ship," so named for the dragon heads carved into the raised prow and stern, might have been "as much as 120 feet [about 36.6 meters] long and able to carry perhaps 80 armed men at a time."[liii] Richard Hall describes a ship excavated at Hedeby as having been "built in c. 985 and was 30.9 m (101 feet) long ... and probably carried about 60 oarsmen."[liv] However, Anders Winroth estimates that smaller ships may have been more commonly used. Winroth describes one ship excavated in Denmark, called *Skuldelev 5*, which was "a little more than eighteen meters [59 feet] long and had space for thirteen pairs of oars."[lv]

Raiding parties might encompass only a handful of ships, but some Viking armies might muster one hundred or more vessels, depending on the objective of the raid. One attack, on Canterbury and the port of London in 851, purportedly was made by 350 ships.[lvi] We don't have any information on the numbers of men carried in these ships, but if we estimate that each ship carried 40 men, the sack of Canterbury would have been accomplished by about 14,000 men. If these ships were of the larger type described by Oliver, those numbers might have been double. Viking warriors were bold, ruthless, and had been trained from a young age to handle weapons, so it is no surprise that the sighting of Viking sails on the horizon or of longships rowing down the river struck terror into the hearts of the people who were unfortunate enough to have been the targets of Viking raids.

Exploration and Colonization

Raiding was only one reason why Vikings sailed to other lands. Vikings also made attempts at colonization, some successful, some not, and some of these attempts also encompassed exploration of new lands beyond the boundaries of medieval Scandinavia. Iceland was first settled by Vikings in the ninth century, while Scandinavian colonies along the Volkhov River—where the Vikings were known as "Rus"—flourished during the Viking Age. Schoolchildren today learn about the exploits of Leif Eiriksson, who attempted a settlement in what is now Newfoundland in Canada. A different Viking incursion, this time into England in 865, was made not with the aim of pillaging and then going home but rather of establishing a permanent Danish colony on English soil.

The Vikings who wished to colonize England were known as the "Great Army" or sometimes the "Great Heathen Army," which was led by men named Ivar, Halfdan, and Ubbe.[lvii] Ivar is usually thought to be Ragnar's son Ivar the Boneless, and Ubbe is named as one of Ragnar's sons in Saxo's *Gesta Danorum*. (The identities of Ragnar's progeny are discussed in more detail in a later chapter.) Neil Oliver states that this army of Vikings numbered about three thousand, and it was a continuous presence in Anglo-Saxon territories for about thirty years.[lviii]

In 878, after the Vikings had fought and pillaged their way through a large swath of English territory, King Alfred of England was finally able to defeat one segment of the Great Army and make a peace treaty with them. The treaty ceded to the Vikings an enormous amount of land that came to be known as the "Danelaw," since these lands were governed under Scandinavian law, not English. The Danelaw's boundaries extended northward from the Thames as far as the border with Northumbria and Strathclyde, and westward and eastward to take up a good portion of central and eastern England. One legacy of the Danelaw can be seen in many English place-names. The particles *-by*, *-thorp* (or *-thorpe*), and *-thwaite* that appear in names such as Whitby ("white homestead"), Scunthorpe ("outlying farmstead that belongs to Skuma"), and Bassenthwaite ("meadow that belongs to the Bastun family") are all of Norse origin.[lix]

While the Danelaw was created in order to stem the violence of an invading Viking army, the Scandinavian settlements that were founded along the Volkhov River appear to have been an outgrowth of Viking trade with the peoples in that region. Archaeological excavations at the settlements of Staraya Ladoga and Novgorod have yielded a great deal of information about these colonies, whose Viking inhabitants were known as "Rus," the word that gives Russia its name.

Staraya Ladoga appears to have been founded sometime in the eighth century, initially as a market center. Excavations there have found items such as a full set of blacksmith's tools, a great deal of glass beads, and dirham coins.[lx] The configuration of burials and burial sites also shows that the Scandinavian population lived side by side with the Slavs who were native to the area. Types of graves, methods of burial, and the creation of separate Scandinavian and Slavic burial grounds all attest to the ways these two peoples lived together over a thousand years ago.[lxi]

Novgorod is a somewhat later settlement than Staraya Ladoga, having been founded in the middle of the tenth century. Medieval Novgorod is also surprisingly well preserved; many of the buildings that made up this medieval town have been unearthed in relatively good condition and are comprised of a mixture of dwellings and workshops. Excavated goods include brooches, amulets, furniture, clothing, toy swords made of wood and, perhaps most importantly, letters that were written on birch bark, which demonstrate that this was a literate population.[lxii]

In Viking settlements along the Volkhov and in the Danelaw, the Scandinavian immigrant population gradually merged with the local ones. The settlement of Iceland was a completely different situation, however, since at the time of the original Scandinavian settlements, Iceland was entirely unpopulated.

Scandinavians began to settle Iceland in the late ninth century. A history of Iceland written in the second quarter of the twelfth century by Icelander Ari Thorgilsson places the start of colonization around 870. Examination of ice core samples taken from Iceland's glaciers appears to corroborate this date, although some controversy exists over the accuracy of the dating method used, which is based on chemical signatures from lava flows.[lxiii] Richard Hall estimates that by

1095, there may have been between 40,000 and 100,000 people living in Iceland, a number he bases on a census taken of people who had the right to attend the *Althing*, Iceland's national assembly, in that year. Hall reports that the 1095 census enumerated 4,560 "free land-owning farmers" as the basis for the estimated total population.[lxiv] Hall does not give the method used for his estimate, but one may assume that it is based on some sort of known proportion of landowners to those who were landless.

The Viking expeditions to what is now Canada did not have the good fortune that had attended many settlements elsewhere. The place that the Vikings dubbed "Vinland," for its supposed wealth of grapevines, was first visited by Vikings as the result of an accident. A man named Bjarni Hejolfsson was sailing from Iceland to Greenland in 986 when he was blown off course and came within sight of what is now Labrador. However, Bjarni did not land there; instead, he turned around and sailed safely to Iceland.[lxv]

Bjarni's tale of his adventure caught the ear of Leif Eiriksson, the son of Eirik the Red, who founded the ill-fated Viking colony in southern Greenland. Eiriksson bought Bjarni's ship, put together a crew, and sailed westward. Leif sailed along the coast of this new land until he found a suitable place for a camp, where he and his crew constructed shelters. Leif called his settlement *Leifsbuthir*.[lxvi]

Although there were several attempts by Leif's brothers and sister to anchor the colony and populate it, nothing ever came of those efforts. Extant sagas, which were penned centuries after the event, tell of difficulties with Indigenous peoples that the Viking settlers called *skraelings*. Eventually, the Vikings gave up on their settlement in this new land. It would be several hundred years before other white settlers went there in search of fishing grounds, timber, and other resources.

For a long time, many modern historians doubted the veracity of the Vinland story. However, Norwegian archaeologist Anne Stine Ingstad worked on excavations throughout most of the 1960s and unearthed undeniable evidence of a Viking presence in a place called L'Anse aux Meadows in Newfoundland. The settlement there is now assumed to be what remains of Leifsbuthir.[lxvii]

Whether operating as traders along rivers or overland, or as raiders pillaging along foreign coastlines, or as explorers seeking new lands, Vikings were a vital presence throughout a significant portion of Europe, Asia, and the Middle East. Medieval Scandinavians brought terror to the places they looted and commerce to the places where they traded. It is impossible to imagine the Middle Ages without Vikings, whose culture and history are a testament to the ways in which the world has always been connected, centuries before our current modes of near-instant communication.

Viking Verbal Arts

Icelandic Sagas and the Sources of the Saga of Ragnar Lothbrok

The word "saga" has entered the modern lexicon as a term that evokes images of great journeys, heroism, epic battles, fantasy, and often a sense of pastness, even if the story itself is not set in either a real or imagined past. However, this is a more modern definition. "Saga," an Icelandic word, originally meant simply "story," "history," or "myth," and it was first used in English as a generic term to describe Scandinavian prose writings in the eighteenth century. The definition with which we are familiar today is the result of expansions of meaning adopted over the nineteenth and twentieth centuries but which ultimately has its basis in the type of stories and characters contained in the Icelandic sagas.

The original corpus of Icelandic sagas began to be compiled in the twelfth century after writing was introduced by missionaries as a part of the Christianization of Scandinavia, whereas previously the sagas had been transmitted orally. Modern scholars have divided the sagas into various genres depending on the content of the stories. In his translation of the Lothbrok saga, author Ben Waggoner notes that these genres are rarely completely watertight: sagas of one type often contain elements that are characteristic of another.[lxviii]

There are three main types of saga: the sagas of Icelanders, which are more or less historical tales about the settlers who first populated Iceland in the Middle Ages; the kings' sagas, which are historical and pseudo-historical stories about Scandinavian kings; and the *Fornaldarsögur*, a term that Waggoner translates as "sagas of old times" but are more commonly known as "legendary sagas." These legendary sagas encompass Germanic myths and heroic legends.[lxix] Waggoner notes that the *Saga of Ragnar Lodbrok* is one of those that defies generic classification since Lothbrok's story combines elements of both the kings' sagas and the legendary sagas.[lxx] This is because Lothbrok is depicted as a king in a pseudo-historical tale that includes such fantasy elements as dragon-slaying and enchanted cows and also because part of Lothbrok's saga draws directly from one of the most important legendary sagas, the *Saga of the Volsungs*, which is discussed in greater detail below. (Appendix A contains a synopsis of the *Saga of the Volsungs*.)

A fourth important source for medieval Scandinavian myths and poetry is the pair of compilations known as the *Prose* (or *Younger*) *Edda* and the *Poetic* (or *Elder*) *Edda*, which were written down by Icelandic historian Snorri Sturluson in the early thirteenth century. The *Poetic Edda* is a collection of Norse myths in poetic form, while the *Prose Edda* is a manual for poetic composition. The *Prose Edda* was Sturluson's attempt to capture and describe the structure and intricacies of the ancient Norse poetry known as skaldic verse. Like the *Poetic Edda*, the *Prose Edda* also contains many Norse myths.

The *Saga of Ragnar Lothbrok* is preserved in multiple manuscript sources, some of which are more complete than others. Waggoner states that the most complete version of the saga is in a manuscript compiled around 1400, which now resides in the Royal Danish Library in Copenhagen and which presents the *Saga of Ragnar Lothbrok* as a direct continuation of the *Saga of the Volsungs*.[lxxi] Waggoner notes that another manuscript in the Royal Danish

Library preserves a slightly different version of Ragnar's story, but unfortunately that manuscript is not complete.[lxxii]

Adjunct to Ragnar's saga proper is the *Tale of Ragnar's Sons*, detailing the deeds and adventures of Ragnar's progeny after their father's death at the hands of King Ella of Northumbria. The primary source for this portion of the story is the so-called *Hauksbók*, a manuscript compiled in the early fourteenth century by Icelander Haukr Erlendson. The *Tale of Ragnar's Sons*, which may have been written by Erlendson himself, is only one of many different items in this manuscript, which Waggoner notes also contains "Christian writings, historical works, and mathematical texts."[lxxiii]

The last main source for Ragnar's story is the *Krákumál*, a 29-stave anonymous poem written in the twelfth century, probably somewhere in the Scottish islands.[lxxiv] The *Krákumál*, or "Kraka's Lay," purports to be Ragnar's death-song, which Ragnar delivers while in a pit full of venomous snakes, where he dies at King Ella's command. The *Krákumál* is written in *háttlausa*, a type of skaldic meter that employs the alliteration common to Germanic and Scandinavian poetry of this period but avoids the internal rhyme of the more formal *dróttkvaett*, or "court meter," about which more is written below.[lxxv] Each stanza of the *Krákumál* begins with a refrain ("We hewed them with our swords") and then goes on to describe Ragnar's exploits in battles with various kings and nobles in various far-flung places, most of which are not mentioned either in the text of the saga proper or in the *Tale of Ragnar's Sons*.

Two other ancillary sources for Ragnar's story are a fragment of an Icelandic saga about Swedish and Danish kings and a sixteenth-century copy of part of the now-lost *Saga of the Scyldings* (*Skjöldungasaga*), a tale about the Danish Scylding dynasty. The Scyldings also appear in the Anglo-Saxon tale *Beowulf*; Beowulf's friend, Hrothgar, is a member of this dynasty. Waggoner states that the fragment of Ragnar's saga having to do with the kings tells the tale of Ragnar's forebears, while the *Saga of the Scyldings* contains material that also appears in the *Tale of Ragnar's Sons*.[lxxvi]

A final source is neither an Icelandic saga nor an Old Norse poem but rather a historical work in Latin, the *Gesta Danorum* ("Deeds of the Danes"), which was written by the medieval Danish historian Saxo Grammaticus (c. 1160-c. 1220). This monumental work, comprised of a series of nine books, is a history of Denmark from ancient times to the twelfth century. It contains a narrative of Ragnar's life and deeds although, as with the saga proper, it is difficult to untangle fact from fiction in Saxo's history.[lxxvii]

Some elements are shared between the saga and *Gesta Danorum*—such as the dragon-slaying episode and the source of the nickname "Lothbrok"—but there are significant variations between these two versions of the life and deeds of Ragnar Lothbrok.[lxxviii] Various details such as the names and number of Ragnar's sons are different in Saxo's account, and some aspects of the plot and action in the *Gesta* are not the same as in the saga proper. For example, Saxo relates battles between Ragnar and "Karl," (presumably Charles the Bald of France, who reigned from 843 to 877), as well as Ragnar's conquest of the Hellespont, neither of which appear in the saga itself.[lxxix]

Ragnar's saga therefore participates both in the fluidity of an oral tradition, in which pieces of a story might vary from transmission to transmission, and also in the very human impulse to ground a story, no matter how fantastic, in a world with qualities familiar to readers and listeners. It also reflects the urge to connect people with the past, whether real or imagined, in an effort to understand how things came to be the way they are.

Skaldic Poetry

Reputation and fame were vitally important to Vikings, and in particular to Viking chiefs and kings. In an age before the advent of writing, one way to broadcast one's deeds was to employ a skald, or court poet, to create songs detailing what one had accomplished.

Skaldic poetry originally was an oral art form, but after the advent of Christianity, it began to be preserved in writing. Extant skaldic poems often are attributed to particular poets and, to a certain extent, can be used as historical sources since they involve descriptions of contemporary events and praise of contemporary dignitaries.[lxxx] These characteristics distinguish skaldic poetry from that found in the Eddas. Eddic poetry, in contrast to skaldic, is usually anonymous and deals with deeds of past heroes or with mythological subjects.[lxxxi]

The most common form used for skaldic poetry is the *dróttkvaett*, or "court meter." This is a complex form with strict rules about line length, syllable stress, alliteration, and rhyme. Each stanza of a poem in court meter has eight lines, which are composed as four sets of *ab* pairs. Each line must have six syllables, three of which must be stressed and three of which must be unstressed. The last syllable of each line must be an unstressed syllable. The *a* line must have two alliterative syllables, and the following *b* line must use that same alliteration on one syllable. Every line also has to have internal rhymes.

In addition to formal poetic structures, skaldic poetry employed an additional layer of complexity in the form of kennings. A kenning is an oblique way of referring to a person or object and has two parts: the base word and the determinant. In her book on Viking life, author Kirsten Wolf presents the example of "surf horse" as a kenning for "ship," where "horse" is the base word naming the object, and "surf" is the determinant that qualifies the base word.[lxxxii] "Surf horse" is a relatively simple and straightforward kenning; often these were significantly more abstruse.

Kennings were used not only to make the poems more complex and therefore more interesting but also to help the skald stick to the rules for the meter by creating additional syllables with their attendant stresses, vowels for rhyming, and initial sounds for alliteration.[lxxxiii] They were also a means by which the skald could show their creativity and skill with words since they had to make up circumlocutions for otherwise ordinary words in addition to fitting everything within the restrictions imposed by the meter. Considering that this poetry originally was composed and transmitted without writing the poems down, it must have taken both a great deal of training and practice, as well as a prodigious memory, to be a skald.

Skaldic poetry has a role to play within the *Saga of Ragnar Lothbrok*. In a few places, Ragnar speaks using skaldic verse, as does Kraka/Aslaug, Ragnar's third wife. Each instance of verse is an example of heightened speech, where the situation calls for something other than mere dialogue. The first of these is when Ragnar kills the dragon that has been keeping the young noblewoman Thora captive. After the dragon is dead, Thora asks the name of her savior, and Ragnar replies with a verse that gives hints about his identity but does not reveal his name. Other skaldic exchanges take place during Ragnar's courtship of Kraka/Aslaug. When Kraka/Aslaug arrives at Ragnar's ships having met the conditions of the riddle Ragnar sets her, she announces her presence in verse. At the end of this first encounter, Ragnar uses skaldic verse to offer Kraka/Aslaug one of his first wife's shirts as a gift. Kraka/Aslaug declines the gift, which is also done in skaldic verse.

These poetic utterances serve two main purposes. One of these is a kind of solemnization of the moment, because the characters break out of normal speech patterns and use highly structured poetic language to convey what they want to say. The other is a revelation of social status: when Ragnar answers Thora's request for his name by using poetry and when Kraka/Aslaug uses poetry to address Ragnar later in the saga, both Ragnar and Kraka/Aslaug are indicating that they are of high social status because they are able to spontaneously construct and deliver skaldic verse, a form of poetry associated with noble and royal courts.

That Ragnar speaks in skaldic verse in the dragon-killing scene is important because it lets Thora know that despite his outlandish dress, her savior is her social equal and therefore it will be possible for Thora to marry him without shame. A similar condition is found in the exchanges between Kraka/Aslaug and Ragnar, where Ragnar's use of skaldic verse indicates his status as king and advertises his intelligence as a quality a woman might want in a husband. Kraka/Aslaug's use of verse also reveals something of her identity by showing that although she appears to be the daughter of peasants, she is in fact of much nobler stock and worthy to be Ragnar's wife and queen to his people. Thora, by contrast, does not need to speak in skaldic verse because her social position and lineage are never hidden and never in question. The same goes for Lagertha, Ragnar's first wife, who is a queen and warrior in her own right.

As we saw earlier, one of the sources for Ragnar's story is the *Krákumál*, or "Kraka's Lay." Evidently the snippets of poetry sprinkled into the saga proper were not enough for the person who composed the lay; they found it necessary to put into Ragnar's mouth an entire, extensive poem detailing his exploits, even going so far as to add adventures to which the saga does not testify. In one sense, then, the *Krákumál* might be seen as an early, poetic form of fan fiction.

Although it is ill-advised to take either skaldic poetry or the sagas at face value as historical sources, they nevertheless provide us with some nuggets of actual history. However, their true worth is not as witnesses to historical events but rather to the worldview of the people who created and compiled these stories. Through sagas and skaldic poetry, we learn which human qualities were most esteemed by the people that produced them, how cultural and social practices were seen and valued, and the skill and breadth of the imaginations of their creators.

Who Was Ragnar Lothbrok?

Like King Arthur and Robin Hood, Ragnar Lothbrok may have been a real person who may have done some of the deeds attributed to him in the sagas and related sources such as the *Krákumál*, and in medieval chronicles that record Viking activities. However, as with

King Arthur and Robin Hood, it is not always easy to separate truth from fiction with respect to Ragnar Lothbrok. Dragon-slaying obviously falls onto the fictional side of things, but Viking raids in England, Norway, and France, and battles with Swedish kings are historically plausible, whether or not they actually happened as described in the saga.

One part of the problem is that sources purporting to be true histories were written down centuries after Lothbrok's supposed lifetime, and another part is the difficulty in figuring out whether the "Ragnar" named in a particular medieval chronicle is the "real" Ragnar Lothbrok (assuming such a person ever existed) or if it was someone else with the same name. Frankish chronicles mention one "Reginheri," who sacked Paris in 845, and a "Reginarius," who received land and a monastery from Charles the Bald in 840, while a Norse king named "Ragnall" is mentioned in Irish chronicles as having invaded Ireland in 851. Because of the paucity of sources and corroborating evidence, it is impossible to say whether any or all of these men were Ragnar Lothbrok. It is also possible that Reginheri, Reginarius, and Ragnall were all separate individuals and that none of them were Lothbrok.

The evidence for the existence of Lothbrok's sons is only slightly less shaky than that for Lothbrok himself. Björn Ironsides appears to have been an actual historical personage, and Sigurd Snake-in-the-Eye may have been as well, although whether they were really the sons of a historical Ragnar Lothbrok is an unanswered question. Ivar the Boneless and his brother Ubbe (mentioned in Saxo Grammaticus' *Gesta Danorum* but not in the saga) are credited by an addition made to one manuscript copy of the late ninth-century *Anglo-Saxon Chronicle* with having led a Viking army that invaded England in 878.[lxxxiv] According to author R. Bartlett, Abbo of Fleury, who wrote around 986, names Ivar and Ubbe as the killers of King Edmund (later St. Edmund the Martyr).[lxxxv] Ivar's and Ubbe's names also appear in a bevy of other later medieval histories of England, whose authors credit them with other depredations such as the destruction of Ely.[lxxxvi]

We may never know whether some of these people actually existed, nor may we ever know what their exact relationship, if any, to the putative Lothbrok may have been. However, we do know that lineage was of vital importance in medieval Scandinavian society and that to be able to claim descent from a famous personage or even from a divine being conferred status. At least one compiler of Ragnar's saga attempted to increase Ragnar's own status and thus the status of his sons through Ragnar's relationship by marriage to the Volsungs, one of the most important families in medieval Scandinavian myths and legends. This family's story is told in the *Saga of the Volsungs*, and it is a tale of dragons, cursed gold, love triangles, battles, and magic that inspired the medieval imagination and later was an important influence on more modern creators, such as opera composer Richard Wagner and author J. R. R. Tolkien.

The version of Ragnar's legend mentioned above treats it not as ancillary to the *Saga of the Volsungs* but rather a direct branching off from it. It takes up where the story of the Volsung Sigurd Fafnirsbane and his beloved Valkyrie Brynhild leaves off, with the escape of Heimer, Brynhild's foster-father, and the child Aslaug after the death of Sigurd and Brynhild, who are Aslaug's parents and two of the most important characters in the *Saga of the Volsungs*. Ragnar eventually takes Aslaug as his third wife, initially not knowing that she is the daughter of Sigurd and Brynhild, since when Ragnar meets her, she is living with peasants and goes by the name Kraka. It is not until much later in Ragnar's saga that Aslaug reveals her true lineage and proves it by saying that her next child will be a boy with a snake in his eye in honor of his maternal grandfather, who killed the dragon Fafnir. Aslaug's prophecy comes true, and the boy is named Sigurd Snake-in-the-Eye.

Not only was it important for Ragnar and his sons by Kraka/Aslaug (Björn, Ivar, Sigurd, and Hvitserk) to be able to claim the connection to the hero Sigurd and his lover Brynhild; it also allowed Ragnar and his children to claim a direct family relationship to Odin the All-Father himself. Volsung, the founder of the Volsung clan, was Kraka/Aslaug's grandfather, while Odin, in turn, was Volsung's great-grandfather. What greater legitimacy can one claim than to be descended from or married into the family of the most powerful god of the Norse pantheon?

Regardless of Ragnar's actual historicity, his character had an important influence on Scandinavian culture and society. Claiming someone like Ragnar Lothbrok as a forebear conveyed a certain amount of personal cachet and legitimacy that one might use to one's advantage. In the introduction to his translation of Ragnar's saga, author Ben Waggoner gives the example of Snorri Sturluson, the twelfth-century compiler of the Icelandic Eddas, who could claim descent from Björn Ironsides.[lxxxvii] Author Jackson Crawford, in his translation of the saga, states that Harald Fairhair (d. c. 930 CE), the first king of the united kingdom of Norway, claimed that Sigurd Snake-in-the-Eye was his grandfather.[lxxxviii]

These sorts of claims did not die with the Middle Ages: they were still being made in more modern times, also with the aim of establishing political and social legitimacy. In 1879, author Albert Welles published a genealogy of American President George Washington, claiming that Washington was a descendant of a man named Odin, whom Welles says assumed the name of that deity later in his life.[lxxxix] Welles' genealogy of course includes Ragnar Lothbrok and his sons among Washington's forebears via Thorfinn the Dane, who according to Welles migrated to England from Denmark in the early eleventh century and settled in Yorkshire, which was then part of the Danelaw.[xc] Of course the accuracy of Welles' genealogy is suspect, at least with regard to the generations before Thorfinn, because Welles uncritically assumes that everyone named in his sources must have been an actual historical person. Nevertheless, it is interesting to note that Ragnar and his progeny are still appearing in politically-motivated genealogies even one thousand years after their lifetimes.

In the end, however—and despite all attempts by others to increase their status by claiming Ragnar as an ancestor—it does not really matter whether the Lothbrok of the saga was an actual historical personage or a composite around whom a complex of legends, both historical and fictional, was woven, or whether he was made up out of whole cloth by an ancient storyteller. Ragnar's saga is a tale worth telling in and of itself, a tale about believable, sympathetic characters and a tale from which we can learn much about Viking culture and society.

[1]Notes to The World of Ragnar Lothbrok

Kirsten Wolf, *Daily Life of the Vikings* (Westport: The Greenwood Press, 2004), p. 22.

[1] Wolf, *Daily Life*, p. 22.

[1] Wolf, *Daily Life*, p. 22.

[1] Richard Hall, *The World of the Vikings* (New York: Thames and Hudson, 2007), pp. 40-43.

[1] Anders Winroth, *The Age of the Vikings* (Princeton: Princeton University Press, 2014), pp. 138-9.

[1] James Graham-Campbell, ed., *Cultural Atlas of the Viking World* (Oxford: Andromeda, 1994), p. 63.

[1] Graham-Campbell, *Cultural Atlas*, pp. 80-83.

[1] Wolf, *Daily Life*, p. 8.

[1] Wolf, *Daily Life*, pp. 10-11.

[1] Wolf, *Daily Life*, pp. 22-24.

[1] Winroth, *Age of the Vikings*, pp. 164-65.

[1] The stories of women warriors in Saxo's history are summarized in Judith Jesch, *Women in the Viking Age* (Woodbridge: The Boydell Press, 1991), pp. 176ff.

[1] Charlotte Hendenstierna-Jonson et al., "A Female Viking Warrior Confirmed by Genomics," *American Journal of Physical Anthropology* 164/4 (2017): 853-60.

[1] Hendenstierna-Jonson et al., "Female Viking Warrior," p. 855.

[1] Hendenstierna-Jonson et al., "Female Viking Warrior," p. 855-57.

[1] Hall, *World of the Vikings*, p. 34.

[1] Jesch, *Women in the Viking Age*, pp. 183-85.

[1] Wolf, *Daily Life*, p. 13.

[1] Wolf, *Daily Life*, pp. 8-9.

[1] Wolf, *Daily Life*, p. 10.

[1] Wolf, *Daily Life*, p. 10.

[1] Winroth, *Age of the Vikings*, pp. 162-64.

[1] Winroth, *Age of the Vikings*, pp. 162-64.

[1] Winroth, *Age of the Vikings*, pp. 163-64.

[1] Neil Oliver, *The Vikings: A New History* (New York: Pegasus Books LLC, 2013), p. 108.

[1] Winroth, *Age of the Vikings*, p. 123.

[1] John Haywood, *Northmen: The Viking Saga AD 793-1241* (New York: St. Martin's Press, 2015), p. 14.

[1] Wolf, *Daily Life*, p. 24; Graham-Campbell, *Cultural Atlas*, p. 75.

[1] Haywood, *Northmen*, pp. 20-22; Graham-Campell, *Cultural Atlas*, p. 75.

[1] Haywood, *Northmen*, p. 22.

[1] Graham-Campbell, *Cultural Atlas*, p. 75.

[1] Graham-Campbell, *Cultural Atlas*, p. 79.

[1] Wolf, *Daily Life*, p. 24.

[1] Graham-Campbell, *Cultural Atlas*, p. 78.

[1] Graham-Campbell, *Cultural Atlas*, p. 78.

[1] Hall, *World of the Vikings*, pp. 33, 99.

[1] Hall, *World of the Vikings*, p. 101.

[1] Hall, *World of the Vikings*, p. 101.

[1] Winroth, *Age of the Vikings*, pp. 124-27,

[1] Graham-Campbell, *Cultural Atlas*, p. 78.

[1] Graham-Campbell, *Cultural Atlas*, p. 85.

[1] Hall, *World of the Vikings*, p. 59.

[1] Hall, *World of the Vikings*, p. 60.

[1] Hall, *World of the Vikings*, p. 60. Ribe is a town in Denmark.

[1] Haywood, *Northmen*, pp. 42-3.

[1] Haywood, *Northmen*, p. 45.

[1] Haywood, *Northmen*, pp. 45, 88.

[1] Haywood, *Northmen*, pp. 169-70.

[1] Haywood, *Northmen*, p. 40.

[1] Winroth, *Age of the Vikings*, p. 136.

[1] Winroth, *Age of the Vikings*, pp. 136-39.

[1] Winroth, *Age of the Vikings*, pp. 136-37.

[1] Oliver, *New History*, pp. 99-100.

[1] Hall, *Vikings*, p. 54.

[1] Winroth, *Age of the Vikings*, p. 75.

[1] Haywood, *Northmen*, p. 47.

[1] Haywood, *Northmen*, p. 50.

[1] Oliver, New History, p. 169.

[1] Caroline Taggart, *The Book of English Place Names: How Our Towns and Villages Got Their Names* (n. p.: Ebury Press, 2011), pp. 15, 82, 269.

[1] Graham-Campbell, *Cultural Atlas*, pp. 190-91; Winroth, *Age of the Vikings*, p. 114.

[1] Graham-Campbell, *Cultural Atlas*, pp. 190-91.

[1] Graham-Campbell, *Cultural Atlas*, p. 192; Hall, *Vikings*, p. 97.

[1] Hall, *Vikings*, pp. 150, 152.

[1] Hall, *Vikings,* p. 151.

[1] Hall, *Vikings*, p. 181.

[1] Hall, *Vikings*, p. 160.

[1] Hall, *Vikings*, p. 161.

[1] Ben Waggoner, trans., *The Sagas of Ragnar Lodbrok* (New Haven: The Troth, 2009), p. xiii.

[1] Waggoner, *Sagas of Ragnar Lodbrok*, p. xi.

[1] Waggoner, *Sagas of Ragnar Lodbrok*, p. xiii.

[1] Waggoner, *Sagas of Ragnar Lodbrok*, p. xxiv. The manuscript in question is Copenhagen, Royal Danish Library, MS NkS 1824b 4to.

¹ This manuscript is Copenhagen, Royal Danish Library, MS AM 147 4to. Waggoner, *Sagas of Ragnar Lodbrok*, p. xxiv.

¹ Waggoner, *Sagas of Ragnar Lodbrok*, p. xxv. Waggoner also notes that the *Hauksbók* was broken up into its constituent pieces, and the pieces were rebound and catalogued separately. The portion containing the *Tale of Ragnar's Sons* now resides in the Arnamagnaean Institute at the University of Copenhagen as MS AM 544.

¹ Robert Crawford, *Scotland's Books: A History of Scottish Literature* (Oxford: Oxford University Press, 2009), n. p., accessed through Google Books <http://google.com/books> 23 March 2020.

¹ n. a., "Teutonic Forms," p. 3 (PDF accessed via https://www.jsicmail.ac.uk, 23 March 2020). The PDF appears to cite Turville-Petre, p. xix, as a source for the definition of *háttlausa* but does not give a bibliographical description beyond the author's surname and page number. It is possible that this information was taken from *Scaldic Poetry* by Gabriel Turville-Petre (Oxford: Clarendon Press, 1976), p. xxix, but I do not have access to this volume and so cannot confirm the accuracy of this assumption.

¹ Waggoner, *Sagas of Ragnar Lodbrok*, p. x.

¹ Oliver Elton, trans. *The Nine Books of the Danish History of Saxo Grammaticus.* 2 vols. (London: Norroena Society, [1905]).

¹ Elton, trans., *Saxo Grammaticus*, vol. 2, pp. 544-5.

¹ Elton, trans., *Saxo Grammaticus*, vol. 2, pp. 550 (Charlemagne episode) and 552-4 (Hellespont episode).

¹ Winroth, *Age of the Vikings*, pp. 134-38.

¹ Wolf, *Daily Life*, p. 55.

¹ Wolf, *Daily Life*, p. 55.

¹ Crawford, *Volsungs*, p. xv.

¹ R. Bartlett, "The Viking Hiatus in the Cult of Saints as Seen in the Twelfth Century," in *The Long Twelfth-Century View of the Anglo-Saxon Past*, edited by Martin Brett and David A. Woodman (Abingdon: Routledge, 2016), p. 18. Bartlett cites the F manuscript of the *Chronicle*, f. 54. "Viking Hiatus," n. 16.

¹ Bartlett, "Viking Hiatus," pp. 17-8.

¹ Bartlett, "Viking Hiatus," p. 18.

¹ Waggoner, *Sagas of Ragnar Lodbrok*, pp. xvi-xvii.

¹ Crawford, *Volsungs*, p. xix.

[1] Albert Welles, *The Pedigree and History of the Washington Family* (New York: Society Library, 1879).

[1] Welles, *Washington*, p. iv.

Part II: The Saga of Ragnar Lothbrok and His Sons

The version of the saga presented here is a compilation taken from various modern translations and retellings of the story of Ragnar's life and deeds and those of his sons. I have not made any attempt to indicate which parts of the story told here come from which portion of the medieval sources; rather, my goal has been to create a coherent narrative that is accessible to modern readers.

The portions of the saga's dialogue that exist as skaldic poetry have been freely rewritten based on modern translations of the Old Norse. I have used both alliteration and kennings in the poetic sections in an attempt to capture something of the flavor of the original Old Norse poetry, but I have not employed actual skaldic poetic form. The kennings for "dragon" in the poem recited by Ragnar are original to the Old Norse, but the kenning for "black" in the poem recited by Kraka/Aslaug is my own addition.

From time to time, the saga presents ideas or images that deserve further explanation. In order to provide greater context for the modern reader, I have appended notes for these items at the foot of the saga.

Ragnar Becomes King

Once there was a king named Sigurd Ring. He had a fair wife named Afhild, and together they had a son named Ragnar. Ragnar grew into a handsome young man, strong and well made in his body.

When Ragnar was fifteen years old, his mother died. After a suitable period of mourning, Sigurd began to look for a new wife. He set his heart upon Alfsol, the daughter of the king of Jutland. Sigurd sent messengers to Jutland, asking for Alfsol's hand. When Alfsol's father heard the message, he scoffed. He said to the messenger, "Take this answer back to your master. Say to him, 'Sigurd Ring may be a great king, but he is an old man. My daughter is worthy of a better husband than one who is likely to die if not on his wedding night then certainly soon thereafter.'"

When Sigurd heard the king of Jutland's reply, he flew into a rage. "An old man am I, with one foot in the grave? The churl who sits upon the throne of Jutland will regret his reply to me. I will make him eat those words at the point of my spear and take his daughter to wife whether he wills it or no."

Sigurd assembled his army and marched upon Jutland. The Jutlanders fought well and valiantly, but they were no match for Sigurd's men. Soon it became clear that Sigurd would be the victor, and rather than allowing him to take Alfsol by force, her father gave her a goblet of poison to drink, and so she died.

After the battle, Alfsol's body was found by Sigurd's men. They carried it carefully back to their king, who began to weep and mourn when he saw that the fair young woman was dead and that she had died by poisoning.

"Fetch my best ship, and build upon it a pyre," said Sigurd. "I will give Alfsol a good funeral, one fit for a queen, even though she did not live to become one."

The ship was pulled up onto the shore, and Alfsol's body was laid upon a pyre as though she had been a queen. Sigurd stood next to the ship as the pyre was kindled. When the mooring line was cut and the ship began to drift out with the tide, Sigurd sprang aboard and stood in the prow.

"If Alfsol could not join me as my wife in this life, I shall join her in death!" cried Sigurd as he drew his sword. "My son Ragnar is a brave and worthy man. Take him now to be your king!" Then Sigurd took the sword and plunged it into his breast. He fell into the flames, and so his body was burned along with Alfsol's.

And so it was that Ragnar became king, even though he was only fifteen years old. The men of his realm quickly learned to respect him, for his judgement was sound and none could match him in battle. Ragnar led his men on many raids and into many battles, and always they came back victorious, with the holds of their ships full of plunder. Ragnar himself escaped every fight without even a scratch, for his mother had woven him a magic shirt that kept him from all harm.

One of Ragnar's many raiding expeditions took him to Norway. When the battles and the raids were done, he and his men found a sheltered spot at which to beach their ships. They were weary and wanted to rest before sailing for home. They made camp and then spent the night on the beach.

In the morning, Ragnar desired to be alone. He took with him his sword and walked through the forest and up one of the many hills that surrounded the beach. The sky was clear, and the sun was bright, and Ragnar delighted in the beauty of the day.

When he reached the crown of one of the hills, Ragnar decided to sit upon the grass and enjoy the peaceful morning. As he looked out over the land, he saw two armies marching toward one another. The armies met and clashed, and soon it began to go very poorly indeed for one side. Ragnar watched more closely and perceived that the losing army was led not by a man but by a woman who showed such skill with her weapons that none could stand against her. Nevertheless, she could not conquer an entire army by her strength alone, and as her warriors fell one by one under the blades of her enemies, she found herself nearly surrounded and hard-pressed.

Ragnar drew his sword and ran to her aid. He fought so fiercely and with such strength that soon he and the woman between them put the other army to flight. Once the battle was over, the woman went to Ragnar and said, "I thank you for your aid. But for you, surely I would also lie dead on the field alongside so many doughty men. My name is Lagertha, and I rule the lands here. May I know your name that I may thank you properly?"

"I am Ragnar, son of Sigurd Ring, and a king among my own people," said Ragnar. "My men and I beached our ships near here. You are most welcome for my help. Never have I seen a shieldmaiden fight with such strength and skill."

"Come back to my stronghold with me," said Lagertha, "and bring your men with you. You will all be my guests at my victory feast."

That night, Ragnar and his men drank and feasted with Lagertha. By the end of the night, Ragnar had fallen in love with Lagertha, who he found to be wise and well-respected by her people. Ragnar proposed marriage, and Lagertha accepted on condition that they remain in her realm. "I would not be an idle consort, content merely to wait upon her royal husband. Here I rule, and here I shall stay."

Ragnar agreed to Lagertha's terms, and they spent three happy years together as husband and wife. At the end of the third year, Ragnar found himself becoming restless. He longed for voyages across the sea and adventures that led to battle and plunder in faraway places.

One day, a messenger came to Ragnar with news that his kingdom was endangered. Ragnar called for his armor and weapons, and caused a ship to be made ready. Then he went to Lagertha and said, "I must return to my own country. I have been away for too long, and now my kingdom is likely to fall. Come with me! Your skill in battle is unmatched, and I would be grateful for your help."

"When we wed, I told you that it was on condition that you remained here," said Lagertha. "I will not leave the throne of my land to become a retainer in yours. You must choose. Either you stay here as my consort, or we part ways forever."

"Then part we must," said Ragnar, "for I cannot forsake my own people. Farewell, and may good fortune smile upon you."

And so it was that Ragnar and Lagertha parted ways, never to see one another again in this world.

Ragnar and the Dragon

Once there was an Earl of Gautland named Herrud, who had a beautiful daughter named Thora. Herrud doted on his daughter. He gave Thora her own house to live in, and a day rarely passed without the earl giving Thora some present or other. One day, Herrud brought his daughter what looked like a small garden snake, which had been given to him by a merchant from a far-off land. The young woman delighted in the creature and made quite a pet of it. But unbeknownst to Thora and her father, the serpent was not a common snake: it was a baby dragon. The serpent continued to grow and grow until finally it was so large it could no longer fit inside Thora's house. It wrapped itself around the house, and because of its great love for Thora, it would allow no one to cross the threshold except the man who fed it a whole ox every day and who brought food and drink and other needful things to the young woman.

"This cannot stand," said the earl. "My daughter is a prisoner in her own home, and there is no warrior among my own people who is able to kill that dread beast. Send messengers throughout all the lands. Tell them that whoever slays that dragon may have my daughter's hand in marriage and a great deal of gold besides."

The messengers were duly sent, and soon one of them arrived at Ragnar's court. The messenger was given an audience with Ragnar, where he explained his errand to the young king.

"I come from the Earl of Gautland," said the messenger. "He seeks a champion to slay the dragon that keeps his daughter prisoner in her own home. The dragon is large and fearsome. Its fangs drip venom, and its very blood will poison anything it touches. There is no one in all of Gautland who has proven himself brave enough to face the beast, so the earl promises the hand of his daughter in marriage, and much gold besides, to whoever can slay the monster and come out of the battle alive."

"Tell me more of the earl's daughter," said Ragnar. "What manner of woman is she?"

"She is the fairest creature upon this earth," said the messenger. "I saw her once with my own eyes through a window of her house. She is comely of face and body, and her hair is golden and soft as silk. Any man would be proud to call her his wife, and doubtless many champions would have already fought to the death for the honor of her hand but for the interference of the dragon."

Ragnar thanked the messenger and ordered that he be given food and drink and a place to rest before going on his way. Then Ragnar began to think of how he might win Thora's hand for himself. He was very young, but he was king, and he knew that every king was in need of a queen. Surely there was no more worthy queen in the world than the daughter of Earl Herrud. Also, Ragnar had an adventurous spirit, and nothing tempted him quite so much as the chance to test his mettle against a fully grown dragon with venomous fangs and poisonous blood. But how to kill the beast without being poisoned himself?

Finally, Ragnar hit upon the solution. He called for breeches and a cloak to be made out of a shaggy goat's hide. When the garments were complete, Ragnar soaked them in pitch. As soon as the pitch had dried, Ragnar sailed for Gautland, bringing his best spear with him. Beaching his ship in a sheltered place that no one was likely to visit, he went ashore secretly, and dressed in his odd, shaggy clothing, he crept silently to Thora's house, where the dragon lay sleeping with its great coils wrapped around the walls.

Before the dragon could rouse itself to fight, Ragnar thrust at it with his spear and then drew the spear out again. The dragon screamed and went to attack, but Ragnar was too quick. Ragnar thrust again with his spear, and this time the point struck bone. Ragnar pulled the shaft of the spear out, but the shaft broke, and the head remained lodged in the dragon's body. As the dragon thrashed and screamed in its death throes, some of its blood splashed upon Ragnar, but he took no hurt because he was well protected by his odd, shaggy clothing. From that day forward, he was known as "Lothbrok," which means "shaggy breeches."

Thora looked out her window just as Ragnar was walking away. She saw that the dragon had been slain, and she rightly guessed that the man outside was the one who had killed it. Thora went out of her house and called to Ragnar. "Are you the one who slew the dragon? Please accept my thanks," she said.

Ragnar turned, and as he did so, Thora noted how very tall and broad he was, and how very strong and handsome.

"Yes, it was I who slew the beast," said Ragnar.

"Who are you?" asked Thora. "Tell me your name."

Ragnar spoke this verse in reply:

Your champion am I, beautiful lady,

Eighteen winters have I walked the earth.[xci]

Though young I am valiant, and vowed

To bring low the land-fish,[xcii]

Dread beast who besets you

With strength and spear

I vanquished the vile worm

Thrusting home to the very heart

Of the heath-salmon.[xciii]

Then Ragnar turned and walked away.

In the morning, Thora told her father that the dragon had been slain, and she took the earl to see its body. The Earl saw the end of the spear shaft sticking out of the beast's hide. He commanded that the end of the spear be removed. It took three strong men to pull it out, and when they finally had it in their hands, the three of them could barely lift it, even when they all tried together. The Earl marveled at this and asked Thora, "Who is this man? Surely he must be a great champion to wield such a mighty weapon. He deserves our thanks, and I have promised him your hand in marriage."

"I don't know who he is, Father," said the young woman. "I asked him his name, but he answered with a riddle and then walked away without saying anything else. All I know about him is that he is eighteen winters old, that he was very oddly dressed, and that he slew the dragon."

The Earl then decided that a great meeting should be held at his court to find out who his daughter's deliverer was. He sent messengers throughout all the lands, telling the champions to assemble and say whether it was they who had slain the dragon or not, and to bring proof that they had done the deed themselves, and not some other.

On the day of the meeting, Ragnar came into the earl's court along with the men of his ship. He brought with him the broken spear shaft, but he did not wear his shaggy clothing, for he did not want the earl's daughter to see him and identify him thereby.

When all the men had assembled in the hall, the earl thanked them for coming and explained what needed to be done. "The dragon that beset my household has been slain by a mighty spear. The head and part of the shaft were left behind in the beast's body. I will bring the head to each of you so that you may say whether it is yours or not. If you claim it, be prepared to prove it by producing the shaft of the spear. Whoever it is that did this deed will have my daughter's hand in marriage and much gold besides, as I have promised."

Then the earl caused the spearhead to be shown to each man in turn. Every one of them denied that it was theirs, even though they longed to say that it was and thus have the earl's daughter in marriage, for she was very beautiful indeed.

Finally, the spearhead was shown to Ragnar. "It is mine," he said. "With that spear, I slew the dragon."

"Prove it," said the earl, "and if you lie, know that it will go ill for you."

Ragnar produced the broken spear shaft, and the other piece was fitted to it. It was obvious that this was the man who had killed the dragon. The Earl proclaimed a great feast to celebrate the death of the beast, the courage and strength of Ragnar, and the marriage of his daughter to such a fine champion. At the feast, Ragnar took Thora to be his wife, and when the feasting was over, he took her to his own country, where they lived happily together for many years. Thora gave Ragnar two sons named Erik and Agnar. They grew into fine young men, both tall, handsome, and strong. None could best them, either in battle or in contests of sport.

A day came when Thora fell gravely ill. In a few days, she was dead. Ragnar mourned her greatly, and his sorrow was so deep that he could not abide to stay in the country where his beloved wife had died. Ragnar turned the rule of his kingdom over to his sons and advisers and then took ship to begin a life of adventure and raiding once again.

Aslaug

The mighty champion Sigurd, who slew the dragon Fafnir, had a daughter named Aslaug by the Valkyrie named Brynhild. At Sigurd's court, there was an exiled king named Heimer, who had been married to Brynhild's sister. Heimer was a gifted poet and harper, and so had been made Sigurd's skald. Heimer was Aslaug's foster-father, as he had been to her mother before her, and he doted on little Aslaug from the time she was a tiny infant.

When Aslaug was three years old, her parents died. Aslaug's father was murdered at the court of King Gjuki, where he then dwelled, and her mother died by her own hand in grief over Sigurd's death. Knowing that Aslaug was in danger from Sigurd's enemies, Heimer ran away with her. He made a large harp and concealed the child within it so that they might wander from place to place without anyone asking questions, since a skald traveling with his harp was nothing to be curious about.

After a long journey, Heimer and Aslaug arrived in Norway at a place called Spangarheith, where there was a lonely farmstead. The people of the farm were an old man named Aki and his wife, an old woman named Grima. Heimer went to the farmhouse and knocked on the door. When Grima answered, she said, "What is it you want? If you are looking for my husband, he is not here, but he will be back soon."

"I look for nothing but a fire to warm myself by and a place to sleep for the night," said Heimer, "and if you could also spare a crust of bread for a wandering skald, I will be most thankful."

"A fire is already kindled on my hearth, and you may sleep in our barn if you like," said the woman. "I have some bread that I baked yesterday that you are welcome to eat."

Heimer thanked the woman and went to sit by the hearth. He set down his harp and began to warm himself while the woman went back to her own work.

Now, when Heimer left Sigurd's court with little Aslaug, he also packed into the harp a quantity of gold and some of the girl's fine dresses, for she would need both when they finally reached a place of safety. Himself he had dressed in poor clothing, as befits a wandering skald, but he had forgotten to take off the lordly ring he wore upon one finger. The old woman caught a glint of gold when Heimer stretched out his hands to the fire, and when she examined his harp more closely, she saw a bit of fine cloth peeking out from the seam of the door that enclosed Aslaug and her belongings. This set the old woman to thinking about how she might relieve the stranger of his gold and fine cloth, but she said nothing to Heimer of what she had seen.

Presently, the old woman showed Heimer to the place where he was to sleep that night and then returned to her house. Not long after that, her husband came home and was angered to find that his dinner had not yet been prepared, for Grima had been dealing with their visitor instead of cooking a meal.

"Do not be vexed, husband," said Grima. "I saw a thing today that will surely bring us the fortune we have lacked. A wandering skald came to the door today, asking for warmth and shelter. I let him sit by the fire. But this is no ordinary skald. He has fine clothing packed away in that harp of his, and he wears a gold ring upon his finger."

"Yes?" said Aki. "What is that to us?"

"Old fool, don't you see?" replied Grima. "This is our chance! If we kill the skald, we can take his gold and his fine raiment and maybe even sell the harp. We'll never want for anything ever again!"

"This is a wicked thing you're planning, Grima," said Aki. "The skald is a guest in our house. It is a truly shameful thing to murder a guest and then rob him. I won't do it."

"Very well," replied the old woman. "Don't help me then. I'll just put you out to pasture, like a broken-down old horse, and take the skald for my husband. Or we could just kill you. The result will be the same in any case. I mean to live well and comfortably, even if you don't."

After a long quarrel, the old woman finally convinced her husband to help her kill Heimer and steal all of his possessions. Aki took up his axe, and then he and Grima crept silently into the barn where Heimer lay fast asleep with his harp by his side. Aslaug remained hidden within, for Heimer was not sure of her safety even among these poor people.

Grima picked up the harp and brought it back to the cottage, while Aki took his axe and struck Heimer a great blow on his head, killing him instantly. Then Aki went back to the cottage, where he found his wife attempting to open the harp. She was having great difficulty, for Heimer had had the harp constructed with a secret catch, and only he knew how to open it. Finally Grima became so frustrated that she took Aki's axe and broke the harp open. Imagine the surprise of the old couple when they found not just gold and fine raiment but also a beautiful young girl with golden hair concealed within!

"Well, this is a fine turn of events," said Aki. "What are we to do now? Are you thinking we should kill the child, too? I'll have you know that I will not harm a hair on her head, no matter how much you plead."

"No, we'll not kill her," said Grima. "We'll keep her. We could use another pair of hands around the farm. We'll just say she's our daughter."

Aki laughed aloud at this. "Have you looked at yourself, woman? Have you looked at me? We are both old and gnarled and ugly, and this child is the fairest I have ever seen. Surely her parents were both noble people. Who will ever believe us?"

"That's of no matter. We'll disguise her. Dress her in rags, cut her hair, smear her with ashes and mud, and she'll look enough like a peasant's child to pass for our own. And it's not like we have many visitors out here." Then Grima turned to the child and said, "What is your name, child?" but Aslaug was too frightened to reply. The old couple terrified her, and she wondered where her beloved Heimer had gone.

And so it was that Aki and Grima adopted Aslaug and raised her as their own. Since Aslaug could not or would not tell the old couple her name, the woman decided to call her Kraka, which means "crow," in honor of her mother, who also bore that name. Aslaug remained with Grima and Aki, and she grew into a lovely young woman. She retained her habit of silence and rarely spoke, even to her foster-parents. Even so, she was clever and canny, and her beauty was matched well by her wits. Aslaug lived with the old couple and worked for them like a slave, for she had no other choice, but never did she forget her parentage, nor did she ever forget how her beloved foster-father had met his death.

Ragnar and Aslaug

Aslaug, who was now called Kraka, was sixteen years old when Ragnar Lothbrok returned to the sea with his companions. They raided far and near, and after one such raid, they beached their ships near Spangarheith, where dwelt Grima and Aki and their foster-daughter. Ragnar told his cooks to take a measure of flour and other things needed to bake bread and to go find a willing cottager or baker who would help them. The cooks did as Ragnar asked, and once everything was assembled, they went looking for someone to help them bake the bread. Soon enough, they came across Grima and Aki's farmstead. They knocked on the door, and Grima answered.

"What is it you want?" she said.

"We are the companions of Ragnar Lothbrok," they replied. "We beached our ships not far from here. We have come to ask for help in baking bread. Now we have told you who we are. What is your name?"

"I am called Grima, and I would gladly help you, but my hands are too gnarled and stiff to knead bread anymore. I will call my daughter, and she will help you."

Now, Kraka had been out in the field tending to the cattle when she spied Ragnar's ships pulled up on the shingle of the beach.

Thinking that some of the men might come to the farmstead, she went and bathed herself and washed her hair, things that Grima had forbidden her to do lest any man come across her and see how very beautiful she was.

Kraka entered the cottage just as the men were beginning to light a fire to bake the bread. When they saw the girl, they could not believe their eyes. They had never seen a woman so beautiful in all their travels.

"Is this young woman your daughter?" asked the men.

"Yes, indeed she is," said Grima.

"How can that be possible? She is the fairest of all women, and you are gnarled and hideous."

"Time has been unkind to me," said Grima. "You should have seen me in my younger days."

Grima told Kraka to help make the bread. Kraka complied, silently. She helped make the dough and knead it. When it was finally set to bake, the men were so entranced by Kraka that they lost track of time, and the bread was burned.

The cooks returned to their ships with the burned bread. When the meal was served later, all the men complained at how burnt the bread was. Ragnar said, "What happened? You are skilled cooks. You have never burnt the bread like this before."

"No, we have never burnt the bread like this before," said the senior cook, "but we had never seen a girl that beautiful before, either."

"Explain this," said Ragnar.

"Well," said the junior cook, "we found a farmstead and asked for help baking bread, as you asked us to do, and the old woman who lived there had her daughter help us. I swear to you I have never seen a lovelier woman in all my days. She was so entrancing that we kept our gaze fixed on her, and in so doing, we burned the bread."

Ragnar scoffed. "No woman has ever been that beautiful. Come now, tell us what really happened."

But the cooks would not change their tale. Finally Ragnar said, "Very well, if she is as lovely as you have said, go back to the farmstead and ask her to come and visit me here, for it is high time I took a wife again. But you must give her this message: say to her, 'Come to meet Ragnar Lothbrok, our king and the captain of the ships, but he commands that you must come neither dressed nor undressed, neither sated nor hungry, nor must you come alone, but no man may come along with you.'"

The cooks went back to the farmstead, where they found Grima and Kraka working together inside the cottage. They told Kraka what Ragnar said she should do. When Grima heard Ragnar's message, she scoffed. "What is he playing at, giving my daughter those ridiculous instructions? I think this king and captain of yours, if he really is both those things, might not be quite all there."

"No, I think there is a sound purpose behind this message, if only we can puzzle it out," said Kraka. Then she said to the cooks, "Thank your king and captain for his invitation. Tell him that I cannot come with you right now but that I will visit him in the morning."

The cooks went back to the ships and gave Ragnar Kraka's answer. During the night, Kraka thought hard about Ragnar's message and how she might do as he had bid. Finally she arrived at a solution and went to sleep.

In the morning, Kraka went to Aki and said, "I would like to borrow your trout net, please."

Aki thought this an odd request, but he gave her the net anyway. Kraka went to her chamber and took off all her clothes. Then she wrapped the net around herself as though it were a dress. When that was done, she went into the kitchen and took a bite of a leek that lay on the table. "Now I am neither dressed nor undressed, and I am neither sated nor hungry." Kraka turned to Aki once again. "Lend me your old dog so that I may not go alone, but with no man accompanying me."

Kraka went to the ships, the old dog trotting by her side. When she arrived, she stood at the edge of the beach and waited. From his ship, Ragnar saw her and called out, "What is your name, and what is your business here?"

Kraka replied:

I came at the command

Of Ragnar, captain and king;

I dared not deny his summons.

See now how I stand here

Both dressed and naked,

A net draped about my form,

And a fine friend at my side,

That I am not alone

Yet no man is with me.

Ragnar told two of his men to go and meet the young woman and bring her to the ship. Kraka said to the messengers when they arrived, "Gladly will I go to meet your captain and king, but only on condition that both I and my companion are guaranteed safety."

The messengers promised safe conduct to Kraka and the dog, and then led her onto the ship. But when Ragnar went to greet Kraka, the dog bit him. When Ragnar's men saw this, they jumped at the dog and killed it.

Kraka stayed on board for a time, conversing with Ragnar. Ragnar saw that Kraka was every bit as wise and clever as she was beautiful, and he longed to have her for his wife. Ragnar asked her to stay with him, but Kraka replied that if she truly had safe conduct, he would let her go in peace.

"Why will you not stay?" said Ragnar. "I am wholly pleased with you, and I love you. I wish you to stay here with me tonight and become my wife."

"I will not stay tonight," said Kraka. "I will not stay at all until you have made one more journey and returned to me in the same mind you are now. For it is possible that once you have sailed away, you will forget all about me, and had I wed you, I would be forsaken."

Ragnar was vexed that Kraka would not stay with him. He tried one last time to get her to stay by presenting her with a beautifully embroidered shirt that had belonged to his beloved Thora, which he carried with him wherever he went in her memory.

As he presented the shirt, Ragnar said:

Take this now, O maiden,

Glittering gift woven well

That once adorned my beloved Thora.

Sewn by her own hand

Have it now for your own!

Take this gift from a king and a captain

The dearest thing he can bestow.

Kraka replied:

A gracious gift indeed

And graciously given;

But not for the poor maid

Is the shimmering shirt of Thora.

More fitting is the coarse tunic

Blackened with soot.

Crow's-wing color[xciv]

Is what Kraka should wear

For herding the beasts

On paths high and low.

Lordly linen is not meet

For the poor man's daughter.

Then Kraka said, "I will now go home, and you will go on your errand. And if, when you return, you still desire me, send word to me, and I will come."

And so Kraka returned to the old couple's cottage, and Ragnar sailed with the first fair wind. After ten months, when Ragnar's journey was done, he returned to Spangarheith and sent his men to fetch Kraka, for he still desired her for his wife. Kraka agreed to go to Ragnar but not until the following morning.

Kraka arose very early. She went to the old couple and asked whether they were awake. When they said they were, Kraka said, "I am leaving, and I will never return. Listen now, for I have this to say to you: I know that you killed Heimer, my foster-father. I know that you stole the gold and the fine garments that he had hidden away, things that were rightfully mine. You have given me a roof over my head and clothes on my back, and although you have not been kind, you have done me no harm. Therefore I will not seek justice for what you have done. But I do wish one thing for you, that the remainder of your days be bad ones and each one worse than the last."

And so it was that Kraka returned to Ragnar's ship, where she was given a fair welcome. Ragnar sailed with Kraka and his men back to his homeland, where a great wedding feast was prepared. At the feast, Ragnar married Kraka and took him for his queen, and they lived many happy years together. Kraka gave Ragnar four fine sons who were named Ivar the Boneless, Björn Ironsides, Hvitserk, and Ragnvald. Ivar was called "the Boneless" because his bones were soft and did not knit properly.[xcv] He could not walk and had to be carried everywhere on a litter. What he lacked in physical strength he made up for in wisdom and cunning, and his brothers and stepbrothers all relied on his good counsel. Björn was named "Ironsides" because his skin was so tough that no weapon could penetrate it. Ragnvald died young, killed in battle in an attack on Whitby that Ivar had planned.

The Feud with King Eystein

There came a time when Ragnar went to visit King Eystein in Uppsala. Ragnar and Eystein were old friends and allies, and so there was much joy when they met at Eystein's court. Eystein had a beautiful daughter named Ingeborg, who had not yet been betrothed to any man. Now, Ragnar's advisers had long been vexed that their queen was the daughter of farmers, and when they saw how beautiful Ingeborg was, they began to speak out against Kraka in the hopes that Ragnar would divorce her and marry Ingeborg instead.

Ragnar had noted the beauty of Ingeborg, and he was swayed by the arguments of his advisers. Eystein also wished his daughter to marry Ragnar. When it came time to sail for home, Ragnar left Uppsala having promised to divorce Kraka and marry Ingeborg.

As Kraka waited at home for her husband to return, she sat in the courtyard under a tree working at some embroidery. While she worked, three birds came and sat in the branches of the tree. The birds then sang this song:

Queen and lady art thou now,

Until king and captain should break his vow

And a new bride place upon the throne.

His heart towards you he turns to stone.

And so it was that Kraka learned of Ragnar's plan to divorce her and marry another instead.[xcvi]

When Ragnar returned home, Kraka pretended that she knew nothing of his intent. She greeted him joyfully as she always did, asking how his visit had gone and how his friends fared. By this time, Ragnar was beginning to feel that he had behaved churlishly in agreeing to marry Ingeborg and put Kraka away, and because of his shame, he was very curt in his answers. This served only to confirm for Kraka what the birds had said to her. Finally Kraka decided to reveal what she knew.

"Why do you intend to divorce me and marry another?" asked Kraka.

"Who told you that?" said Ragnar, for only he and his closest advisers knew of this plan, and they had only just returned home.

"Three birds I have who are friendly to me. When you go on journeys, I send them to follow you so that they may bring me news. While I sat in the courtyard at my embroidery, they came and sang to me that you wish to have another woman in my place. Why would you want to do that? What ill have I done to you to make you wish to send me away?"

"No ill have you done, but your lowly birth counts against you," said Ragnar. "My advisers grow restless at having a peasant for a queen."

"Then tell your advisers that they are badly mistaken and that no peasant sits upon the throne but rather the daughter of Sigurd Fafnirsbane and the Valkyrie Brynhild," said Kraka.[xcvii] "You found me living among peasants, but those people are not my parents. When I was but a very small child, my foster-father, King Heimer, spirited me away from my father's court to keep me safe from the men who had killed my father. Heimer hid me inside his harp, along with some valuables, and took to the road in search of a place where we might live in peace.

"One day we came to Grima and Aki's farmstead, where Heimer asked for shelter. Grima and Aki killed my foster-father for the gold and fine garments he carried within his harp. When they broke open the harp to get at the valuable things, they also found me there. The old people adopted me and kept me as their own, but I am none of their blood. A daughter of the Volsungs am I, well fit to be your queen. My true name is Aslaug."

"An astonishing tale to be sure," said Ragnar, "but what proof have you that this is true? For proof I must have if I am to convince my advisers and if I am to break my betrothal to Ingeborg, daughter of King Eystein."

"Two things Grima and Aki allowed me to keep when they found me," said Aslaug. "One is my mother's wedding ring. The other is a letter my mother wrote to me before she died. Also, I have found myself again with child. When the child is born, it will be a boy, and he will have the image of a serpent in one of his eyes as a token of his relation to my father, who slew the great dragon Fafnir."

Aslaug then produced the ring and the letter, and when her time came to be delivered of her child, she gave birth to a boy who had the image of a serpent in one eye. The child was named Sigurd Snake-in-the Eye in honor of his grandfather and on account of the marking in his eye.

Ragnar saw all these tokens and begged forgiveness of Aslaug. Then he sent word to Eystein that he must break his betrothal to Ingeborg. And thus it was that Ragnar and Eystein, who had been friends from of old, became sworn enemies. This enmity would prove to be the undoing of Agnar and Erik, Ragnar's sons by his first wife, Thora.

When Ragnar went back on his promise to wed Ingeborg, Eystein vowed revenge. Eystein summoned his army with the intent of marching to Denmark and taking Ragnar's stronghold. As soon as word arrived of what Eystein purposed to do, Ragnar mustered his men and prepared to go to war, but Agnar and Erik asked to be sent at the head of the army in Ragnar's place.

"We are men full grown, Father," said Agnar. "Give us the honor of leading your army into battle. We lack nothing in strength or skill, and we wish only to return victorious as you have done many a time."

Ragnar gave his sons his blessing. Agnar and Erik went forth with Ragnar's army, and in time they met Eystein and his warriors as they were marching toward Denmark. There was a great and fierce battle. Agnar and Erik acquitted themselves well and slew many, but their army was thrown into disarray by an enchanted cow that Eystein loosed in their midst. Soon all was lost, for not only had Ragnar's army been thrown into confusion by the cow, but they were also overwhelmed by the greater numbers of warriors in Eystein's army.

When the battle was finally done, Agnar lay dead on the field, while Erik and a great part of Ragnar's army had been captured by Eystein.

"A bold and skilled warrior are you," Eystein said to Erik. "I would have peace between us. Take my daughter to wife, and you may stay here in my country. Great riches will be yours."

"No peace can there be between us," said Erik. "You slew my brother; I saw his body on the field. Keep your daughter, and keep your riches. All I ask is that my father's men be allowed to go home in safety and a nest of spears be planted in the ground for me that I may join my brother in death."

Eystein saw that Erik was not to be swayed, so he ordered that Ragnar's warriors be allowed to travel home unmolested and that a nest of spears be made with the shafts planted in the ground and the points facing upward. When the spears had been planted, Erik took the ring from his hand and gave it to one of his men. "Take this ring home to my stepmother," he said, "and tell her and my stepbrothers how the sons of Thora died." Then Erik threw himself upon the points of the spears and so perished.

When Ragnar heard what had happened in Sweden, he was enraged by the defeat of his army, and even more so by the deaths of his two eldest sons. Aslaug likewise mourned Agnar and Erik as though they had been her own. Ivar and Björn went before their father and begged his blessing to go to Sweden and avenge their stepbrothers' deaths. Ragnar gladly granted them leave, and so they sailed with the next fair wind, having assembled a great body of picked warriors known for their courage and skill.

When the day of the battle arrived, Eystein once again loosed his enchanted cow into the ranks of Ragnar's men. Again the army was thrown into disarray, but Ivar was not dismayed. Although Ivar could not walk, he was still a redoubtable archer, and in this battle, he showed both his skill and his coolheadedness. As the enchanted cow plunged up and down, scattering Ragnar's warriors, Ivar fitted an arrow to the string and loosed a deadly shot, killing the cow instantly. Once the cow's enchantment had been dispelled, Ragnar's men rallied. Soon the Swedish warriors were put to flight, and Eystein was killed as he ran away from the field. Thus were the sons of Thora and Ragnar Lodbrok avenged.

The Death of Ragnar Lothbrok

When the battle with Eystein was over, Ragnar's remaining sons took ship and went raiding. They sailed southward, capturing town after town and laying waste to village after village. Finally they reached the central coast of Italy, where they thought to raid a city called Luna. They beached their ships within view of the town, and all the townsfolk scurried to secure their gates and garrison their walls in expectation of a Viking assault.

Now, the captain of the Viking ships was a man named Hastein, who was both clever and a skilled warrior, well trusted by Ragnar's sons, and foster-father to Sigurd Snake-in-the-Eye. When the Vikings saw that Luna was too well defended to capture by a direct attack, Hastein came up with a cunning plan instead. Messengers were sent into the town with instructions to say that the Vikings had no intention of raiding. They told the leaders of the town and its church that their captain, a man named Hastein, had fallen gravely ill and wished to be baptized as a Christian before he died. A priest was dispatched to the Viking ships in order to give the sacrament to Hastein, who pretended to be fully converted and to accept Christ as his god.

A few days after Hastein's supposed conversion, the Vikings sent word to the town saying that their captain had died. They told the town leaders that Hastein wished for a funeral Mass with Christian burial and that he had left all his fortune to the church in Luna. Thinking that since the Vikings had not yet shown any wish to attack the town they would continue to behave peacefully, the governor of the town gave leave to the Vikings to bring Hastein's coffin into the city gates and to attend the funeral Mass.

Little did the governor know that Hastein was fully alive inside his coffin and that the Vikings had no intention of leaving without plundering the town. In accord with Hastein's plan, the Vikings made a grand funeral procession into the church, where Hastein's coffin was laid upon a bier. But once the church doors were closed and the Mass began, Hastein kicked open the coffin and sprang out, sword drawn. The other Vikings drew the weapons they had concealed within their clothing, and thus they slew all the worthies of the town. Then they ran out of the church to sack and set fire to the houses.

After the sack of Luna, Ragnar's sons laid waste to many other towns. Soon word of their exploits was carried back to Ragnar's court.

"I must take ship again," Ragnar said. "I will have no one say that Ragnar's sons are more valiant than their father."

Now, many years ago, Ragnar had invaded England and made devastating raids all through the country. Ragnar had demanded tribute from the king as the price of peace, but once Ragnar sailed home, the king had refused to pay it. Ragnar deemed an expedition to exact the tribute to be a chance for glory that would rival that of his sons, and so he caused two ships to be made, each large enough to carry a great host. When Aslaug saw what Ragnar was doing, she feared for the success of his raid. "Husband," she said, "would it not be better to sail with many smaller ships rather than two large ones?"

"Perhaps," Ragnar answered, "but no man has ever conquered England with only two ships, and I mean to be the first one to do it. Think of the songs that will be sung! My fame will be everlasting."

Aslaug tried and tried to sway her husband, but Ragnar stood firm. Finally Aslaug realized it was futile to argue with him. She went to the chest where she kept her dearest treasures, and from it she took a magic shirt that she had woven from her own hair and that had been made without any seams.

"Since your course is not to be altered, take this shirt with you," said Aslaug. "Wear it into battle. It will protect you from all wounds, and then maybe you will be able to return home to me."

When the ships were made and provisioned and the army assembled, Ragnar sailed for England, but his voyage was ill-fated from the start. As Ragnar's ships approached the coast, a great storm blew up, and the ships foundered on the rocks not far from the beach. Undaunted, Ragnar and his men made their way onto land, where they began raiding every village and hamlet that stood in their path.

Word of the Viking attacks came to King Ella. He assembled a great host and went out to meet Ragnar's army, intending to crush it thoroughly before it could do any more damage. The English had the greater host by far, so the battle was decided quickly in Ella's favor. Most of Ragnar's men were killed, and Ragnar himself was taken prisoner.

Ragnar was bound and taken before the king. "Tell us your name and your station," Ella demanded, but Ragnar refused to answer.

"If you will not answer," said Ella, "you will be thrown into a pit of venomous serpents. I ask you again: what is your name and your station?"

Ragnar kept his silence, so Ella did as he said he would do. Ragnar was taken and thrown into a deep pit in which there were many venomous snakes.[xcviii] The snakes tried to bite Ragnar, but they were not able to pierce his skin because of the magic shirt Aslaug had given him. When the English realized why Ragnar was not yet dying, they stripped the shirt from him and left him to his fate.

Without the shirt, the serpents were able to sink their fangs into Ragnar's flesh. Soon Ragnar felt the venom coursing through his veins and knew his death was very near. As he was dying, Ragnar sang his death-song:

Battles fifty and one fought I.

Fearless, dauntless, countless foes I have slain;

My sword shone red with their blood

And the dragon feared my spear-point.

Now death deals its blow to me,

My bane not battle-borne but a writhing worm.

Now Valhalla awaits, the warrior's paradise;

Odin-sent Valkyries descend to take me home.

How the sons of Aslaug will rage

When they find how their hero-father met his doom.

Odin calls me now, ale-cups brimful in his halls.

Dying I sing the song of my deeds;

I laugh as life drains away.[xcix]

When Ella heard Ragnar sing of the sons of Aslaug, he realized who it was that had been thrown into the pit. He ordered Ragnar to be taken out with all haste, hoping that it would be possible to save him and thus avoid the wrath of his sons, but it was too late. Ragnar was already dead by the time his body was brought up out of the pit. Thus ended the life of Ragnar Lothbrok, king, hero, and dragon's bane.

The Revenge of Ragnar's Sons

Now that Ragnar Lothbrok was dead, Ella sent messengers to inform Ragnar's sons. "Mark well how each one takes the news," said Ella, "and bring that information back to me."

Ragnar's sons had arrived home from their own voyaging while their father was away in England. The messenger found the young men taking their ease in the great hall of Ragnar's stronghold. Ivar sat on Ragnar's throne, while Hvitserk and Sigurd played chess. Björn also was there, whittling a spear shaft so that a head might be fitted to it.

As the messenger told the tale of Ragnar's last battle, of his death in the snake pit, and of his last song, Ivar sat cold and unmoving on the throne, listening to every detail and occasionally asking questions of the messenger. The only sign of Ivar's distress was the change of color in his cheeks, which shifted from pallor to redness. Björn, however, grasped the spear shaft in his hands and broke it in two. Hvitserk picked up a chess piece and squeezed it in his hand so hard that the piece shattered and his nails were driven into the flesh, drawing blood. Sigurd, who had been paring his nails with a knife, paid no attention to what he was doing with the blade and so cut his finger to the bone.

When the messenger was done with his tale, Björn said, "Strike down this dog where he stands. No man should live who has seen the death of Ragnar Lothbrok."

"Stay, Björn," said Ivar. "The messenger came in peace, having been sent by his king. He has done his duty, and now he will be allowed to return home in peace."

The messenger left Ragnar's court and returned to England, where he told Ella all that had happened while he delivered his message.

"Ivar is the one we have to fear," said Ella once he had heard all, "although the others surely are dangerous enough in their own right. Set a guard on our eastern coast, and bring news with all speed if Viking sails are on the horizon."

At Ragnar's court, the brothers debated what was to be done.

"Let us take ship with every man who can bear arms and teach Ella a lesson he will not forget!" said Hvitserk.

"Yes, indeed!" said Björn. "We must have vengeance, and Ella will pay with his blood and the blood of many others besides!"

"Yes, Ella must pay," said Ivar, "but why not ask of him wergild and be done?ᶜ Ragnar was told at the time of his sailing that leaving with only two ships was folly, and now he has suffered the fate that was foretold. Why should more good men die for Ragnar's ill choices?"

"Wergild is the coward's vengeance," said Sigurd. "I agree with Hvitserk and Björn. Let us take ship and sail for England as soon as may be."

In the end, the brothers took ship with as many warriors as they could muster. Ivar went along with them, but he refused to take part in the battle. The battle was quickly decided in Ella's favor, and Hvitserk, Björn, and Sigurd were taken captive.

When Ivar learned of the course of the battle and his brothers' fates, he went before Ella to plead for their release. "In recompense for the death of our father, let my brothers return home in safety," said Ivar, "and also give me a small wergild: the amount of land that I might compass within an oxhide. I will remain here in England, and I vow never to take arms against you while I live."

Ella agreed to these terms, thinking the wergild Ivar requested to be both odd and so small as to be laughable, although he did not say so at the time. Hvitserk, Björn, and Sigurd sailed home, while Ivar remained behind in England. Ivar did indeed take a piece of land encompassed by an oxhide, but when Ivar had finished placing the hide, Ella was no longer laughing. Crafty Ivar took the oxhide and had it made soft and pliable, then stretched it out to its greatest extent. When the hide was well stretched, he cut it into the thinnest of strips. Then he took the strips and sewed them end on end in a great circle. Ivar took the circle of oxhide and placed it around a large piece of land, on which he built a stronghold and founded a town called Lundunaborg.ᶜⁱ

Ivar managed his affairs well and befriended all of the nobles in the lands around, treating them even better at his own court than they had been at Ella's. Ivar also pretended to be at peace with Ella and acted toward him as a willing friend and adviser. Soon Ella had been soothed into complacency and Ivar had a great many well-placed friends who were ripe for rebellion. Ivar urged the English nobles to rise up and take the throne from Ella, for Ivar had never forgiven the king for Ragnar's death, and he still intended to make Ella pay dearly for it.

Once all was ready, Ivar sent word to his brothers to muster their armies and sail for England. The brothers and their warriors arrived, and with the aid of Ivar's English friends, they brought battle to Ella. Ella's army was caught by surprise, and its numbers had been badly depleted by the defection of so many nobles. Ella himself was captured and put to death by having the image of an eagle in flight carved into his back with a knife.[cii]

Their vengeance accomplished, Hvitserk, Björn, and Sigurd returned home and divided their father's kingdom among them. Björn took the parts that were in Sweden, while Sigurd ruled in Denmark. Hvitserk continued to sail on voyages, looking for plunder, until he was taken captive and executed. Ivar remained in England, where he had established a Viking colony in Northumbria.

Thus ends the saga of Ragnar Lothbrok and his sons.

Notes to The Saga of Ragnar Lothbrok and His Sons

Kirsten Wolf, *Daily Life of the Vikings* (Westport: The Greenwood Press, 2004), p. 22.

[1] Wolf, *Daily Life*, p. 22.

[1] Wolf, *Daily Life*, p. 22.

[1] Richard Hall, *The World of the Vikings* (New York: Thames and Hudson, 2007), pp. 40-43.

[1] Anders Winroth, *The Age of the Vikings* (Princeton: Princeton University Press, 2014), pp. 138-9.

[1] James Graham-Campbell, ed., *Cultural Atlas of the Viking World* (Oxford: Andromeda, 1994), p. 63.

[1] Graham-Campbell, *Cultural Atlas*, pp. 80-83.

[1] Wolf, *Daily Life*, p. 8.

[1] Wolf, *Daily Life*, pp. 10-11.

[1] Wolf, *Daily Life*, pp. 22-24.

[1] Winroth, *Age of the Vikings*, pp. 164-65.

[1] The stories of women warriors in Saxo's history are summarized in Judith Jesch, *Women in the Viking Age* (Woodbridge: The Boydell Press, 1991), pp. 176ff.

[1] Charlotte Hendenstierna-Jonson et al., "A Female Viking Warrior Confirmed by Genomics," *American Journal of Physical Anthropology* 164/4 (2017): 853-60.

1 Hendenstierna-Jonson et al., "Female Viking Warrior," p. 855.

1 Hendenstierna-Jonson et al., "Female Viking Warrior," p. 855-57.

1 Hall, *World of the Vikings*, p. 34.

1 Jesch, *Women in the Viking Age*, pp. 183-85.

1 Wolf, *Daily Life*, p. 13.

1 Wolf, *Daily Life*, pp. 8-9.

1 Wolf, *Daily Life*, p. 10.

1 Wolf, *Daily Life*, p. 10.

1 Winroth, *Age of the Vikings*, pp. 162-64.

1 Winroth, *Age of the Vikings*, pp. 162-64.

1 Winroth, *Age of the Vikings*, pp. 163-64.

1 Neil Oliver, *The Vikings: A New History* (New York: Pegasus Books LLC, 2013), p. 108.

1 Winroth, *Age of the Vikings*, p. 123.

1 John Haywood, *Northmen: The Viking Saga AD 793-1241* (New York: St. Martin's Press, 2015), p. 14.

1 Wolf, *Daily Life*, p. 24; Graham-Campbell, *Cultural Atlas*, p. 75.

1 Haywood, *Northmen*, pp. 20-22; Graham-Campell, *Cultural Atlas*, p. 75.

1 Haywood, *Northmen*, p. 22.

1 Graham-Campbell, *Cultural Atlas*, p. 75.

1 Graham-Campbell, *Cultural Atlas*, p. 79.

1 Wolf, *Daily Life*, p. 24.

1 Graham-Campbell, *Cultural Atlas*, p. 78.

1 Graham-Campbell, *Cultural Atlas*, p. 78.

1 Hall, *World of the Vikings*, pp. 33, 99.

1 Hall, *World of the Vikings*, p. 101.

1 Hall, *World of the Vikings*, p. 101.

1 Winroth, *Age of the Vikings*, pp. 124-27,

1 Graham-Campbell, *Cultural Atlas*, p. 78.

1 Graham-Campbell, *Cultural Atlas*, p. 85.

1 Hall, *World of the Vikings*, p. 59.

1 Hall, *World of the Vikings*, p. 60.

[1] Hall, *World of the Vikings*, p. 60. Ribe is a town in Denmark.

[1] Haywood, *Northmen*, pp. 42-3.

[1] Haywood, *Northmen*, p. 45.

[1] Haywood, *Northmen*, pp. 45, 88.

[1] Haywood, *Northmen*, pp. 169-70.

[1] Haywood, *Northmen*, p. 40.

[1] Winroth, *Age of the Vikings*, p. 136.

[1] Winroth, *Age of the Vikings*, pp. 136-39.

[1] Winroth, *Age of the Vikings*, pp. 136-37.

[1] Oliver, *New History*, pp. 99-100.

[1] Hall, *Vikings*, p. 54.

[1] Winroth, *Age of the Vikings*, p. 75.

[1] Haywood, *Northmen*, p. 47.

[1] Haywood, *Northmen*, p. 50.

[1] Oliver, New History, p. 169.

[1] Caroline Taggart, *The Book of English Place Names: How Our Towns and Villages Got Their Names* (n. p.: Ebury Press, 2011), pp. 15, 82, 269.

[1] Graham-Campbell, *Cultural Atlas*, pp. 190-91; Winroth, *Age of the Vikings*, p. 114.

[1] Graham-Campbell, *Cultural Atlas*, pp. 190-91.

[1] Graham-Campbell, *Cultural Atlas*, p. 192; Hall, *Vikings*, p. 97.

[1] Hall, *Vikings*, pp. 150, 152.

[1] Hall, *Vikings,* p. 151.

[1] Hall, *Vikings*, p. 181.

[1] Hall, *Vikings*, p. 160.

[1] Hall, *Vikings*, p. 161.

[1] Ben Waggoner, trans., *The Sagas of Ragnar Lodbrok* (New Haven: The Troth, 2009), p. xiii.

[1] Waggoner, *Sagas of Ragnar Lodbrok*, p. xi.

[1] Waggoner, *Sagas of Ragnar Lodbrok*, p. xiii.

[1] Waggoner, *Sagas of Ragnar Lodbrok*, p. xxiv. The manuscript in question is Copenhagen, Royal Danish Library, MS NkS 1824b 4to.

[1] This manuscript is Copenhagen, Royal Danish Library, MS AM 147 4to. Waggoner, *Sagas of Ragnar Lodbrok*, p. xxiv.

[1] Waggoner, *Sagas of Ragnar Lodbrok*, p. xxv. Waggoner also notes that the *Hauksbók* was broken up into its constituent pieces, and the pieces were rebound and catalogued separately. The portion containing the *Tale of Ragnar's Sons* now resides in the Arnamagnaean Institute at the University of Copenhagan as MS AM 544.

[1] Robert Crawford, *Scotland's Books: A History of Scottish Literature* (Oxford: Oxford University Press, 2009), n. p., accessed through Google Books <http://google.com/books> 23 March 2020.

[1] n. a., "Teutonic Forms," p. 3 (PDF accessed via https://www.jsicmail.ac.uk, 23 March 2020). The PDF appears to cite Turville-Petre, p. xix, as a source for the definition of *háttlausa* but does not give a bibliographical description beyond the author's surname and page number. It is possible that this information was taken from *Scaldic Poetry* by Gabriel Turville-Petre (Oxford: Clarendon Press, 1976), p. xxix, but I do not have access to this volume and so cannot confirm the accuracy of this assumption.

[1] Waggoner, *Sagas of Ragnar Lodbrok*, p. x.

[1] Oliver Elton, trans. *The Nine Books of the Danish History of Saxo Grammaticus*. 2 vols. (London: Norroena Society, [1905]).

[1] Elton, trans., *Saxo Grammaticus*, vol. 2, pp. 544-5.

[1] Elton, trans., *Saxo Grammaticus*, vol. 2, pp. 550 (Charlemagne episode) and 552-4 (Hellespont episode).

[1] Winroth, *Age of the Vikings*, pp. 134-38.

[1] Wolf, *Daily Life*, p. 55.

[1] Wolf, *Daily Life*, p. 55.

[1] Crawford, *Volsungs*, p. xv.

[1] R. Bartlett, "The Viking Hiatus in the Cult of Saints as Seen in the Twelfth Century," in *The Long Twelfth-Century View of the Anglo-Saxon Past*, edited by Martin Brett and David A. Woodman (Abingdon: Routledge, 2016), p. 18. Bartlett cites the F manuscript of the *Chronicle*, f. 54. "Viking Hiatus," n. 16.

[1] Bartlett, "Viking Hiatus," pp. 17-8.

[1] Bartlett, "Viking Hiatus," p. 18.

[1] Waggoner, *Sagas of Ragnar Lodbrok*, pp. xvi-xvii.

[1] Crawford, *Volsungs*, p. xix.

[1] Albert Welles, *The Pedigree and History of the Washington Family* (New York: Society Library, 1879).

[1] Welles, *Washington*, p. iv.

[1] In one medieval version of the saga, Ragnar states that he is fifteen years old in his verse to Thora, but this version does not include Ragnar's sojourn with Lagertha. Because I am including the story about Ragnar meeting and marrying Lagertha prior to his encounter with the dragon, I have changed Ragnar's age to eighteen to take his three years with Lagertha into account.

[1] A kenning for "dragon."

[1] Another kenning for "dragon."

[1] A kenning for "black." This is also a play on the name "Kraka," which itself means "crow."

[1] The original sources are unclear about what the exact nature of Ivar's disability was. In some ways, the descriptions seem to suggest a milder form of brittle bone disease (*osteogenesis imperfecta*), but they could also refer to rickets. Rickets is a childhood ailment that leads to a softening of the bones, which is caused by a lack of vitamin D. Effects of this softening include bow-leggedness and knock knees, which impairs one's ability to walk. Rickets is more common in northern latitudes because of the lack of sunlight during a significant part of the year. It can also be caused by genetic factors or by the mother having a severe vitamin D deficiency during pregnancy.

[1] Kraka/Aslaug's father also had the ability to understand the speech of birds, which he acquired by accidentally tasting some of the dragon Fafnir's blood while roasting its heart for Regin, the blacksmith to whom Sigurd was apprenticed and who was the brother of Fafnir.

[1] "Fafnirsbane" means "Killer of Fafnir."

[1] Although the saga was only written down in Christian times, one wonders whether the pit of snakes was intended to be some kind of reference to the pagan concept either of Hvergelmir or of Nastrandir. The latter was a place in the Norse underworld that was made out of venomous serpents, and the former was a place inhabited by a giant serpent. Nastrandir was the place to which the souls of oathbreakers and murderers were consigned and Hvergelmir the place where the souls of the most wicked were consumed by the giant serpent. If this coincidence of imagery between pagan beliefs and the saga's text were in fact intended, it may add yet more degradation to the method used for Ragnar's death since it signals that Ella finds him to be not a noble enemy but rather a dishonorable murderer. It is also possible that a link was intended to be made between Ragnar and Gunnar from the *Saga of the Volsungs*, who also meets his end in a pit of snakes.

[1] This is a significantly shortened version of the *Krákumál*, a 29-stave poem purported to be Ragnar's death-song. In fact, the *Krákumál* is a twelfth-century creation, probably written somewhere in the Scottish islands.

[1] Payment of wergild was an important practice in ancient Germanic and Scandinavian societies. The purpose of wergild was to compensate a victim—or the victim's family, if the victim had been killed—for the hurt they had received through the perpetrator's commission of a crime. The amount to be paid varied depending on the nature of the injury and the gender and social status of the parties concerned. Once wergild had been paid, the victim and/or their family had to relinquish any right to exact further payment or vengeance.

[1] Some of the sources I consulted said that "Lundunaborg" was London; others said that it was Lincoln. Neither identification can be historically accurate since both London and Lincoln were founded by the Romans long before the Vikings ever arrived in England. Peter Munch is in the "London" camp in his *Norse Mythology: Legends of Gods and Heroes* (New York: American-Scandinavian Foundation, 1926), p. 251. Katharine F. Boult, on the other hand, claims that Ivar's stronghold was Lincoln. *Asgard & the Norse Heroes* (London: J. M. Dent & Sons, Ltd., [1914]), p. 253.

[1] The medieval sources do not agree on exactly what Ella's torture and death entailed. Some seem to indicate that the image of an eagle was carved into his back, but another version states that the "eagle" was created by cracking open the victim's rib cage from the back and then splaying his lungs out as though they were wings. Historian Anders Winroth says that the difficulty in translating the original Old Norse has led to other misunderstandings of the "blood eagle." Winroth says that the interpretation in which an eagle is carved into Ella's back with a knife likewise may be a mistranslation, although he finds it grammatically correct, and that it might have been the saga creator's original intent to say that Ella was killed and then his body left as food for birds of prey. *The Age of the Vikings* (Princeton: Princeton University Press, 2014), pp. 36-7.

Part III: Representations of Norse Myths and History in Modern Media

Dragons in Tolkien's Middle-Earth

J. R. R. Tolkien's *The Lord of the Rings* and *The Hobbit, or There and Back Again* have captured the imaginations of readers since their initial publication in the middle of the twentieth century, and have been brought to an even wider audience by Peter Jackson's recent film adaptations. Tolkien's voluminous writings about Middle-earth, its history, and its inhabitants opened up new worlds for generations of his fans and inspired many other writers.

Just as Tolkien's writings became a spur for creators who followed him, ancient Norse and Anglo-Saxon myths were among Tolkien's own inspirations and are deeply woven into his fiction. Tolkien did not generally distance himself from his sources; rather, he was happy to claim that "[i]n the Lord of the Rings, I have tried to modernize the myths and make them credible."[ciii]

Tolkien's exposure both to ancient Norse myths and to Anglo-Saxon literature came early in his life, as did his interest in constructed languages. When Tolkien was a young child, he read

Andrew Lang's version of the *Saga of the Volsungs* in the *Red Fairy Book*, and around the same time, he made his first experiments with constructed languages.[civ] In his teens, Tolkien was a pupil at King Edward's School in Birmingham, where he studied Anglo-Saxon and began teaching himself to read Old Norse.[cv] Old Norse became his special subject in his undergraduate studies at Oxford, as an adjunct to his primary concentration, which was on a linguistic study of English.[cvi]

This interest in languages and Norse and Anglo-Saxon literature alike would create the arc of Tolkien's professional life, the bulk of which was spent at Oxford University, where he was the Rawlinson and Bosworth Professor of Anglo-Saxon and a Fellow of Pembroke College between 1925 and 1945, while from 1945 to 1959 he was the Merton Professor of English Language and Literature and a Fellow of Merton College.[cvii] It was during his tenure at Oxford and in his retirement thereafter that Tolkien wrote *The Hobbit*, *The Lord of the Rings*, and other tales set in Middle-earth, the last of which were published by Tolkien's son, Christopher, after the elder Tolkien's death in 1973.

The connections between Tolkien's works and Norse mythology are complex and extensive enough to fill a book of their own, so I am going to narrow my focus to the matter of dragons in these two bodies of literature. Just as dragons are important figures in *Beowulf* and in the Icelandic sagas, including Ragnar's own, so too do they abound in Tolkien's works, from the terrifying Ancalagon the Black and the deadly, wingless Glaurung in *The Silmarillion*, to glittering Smaug in *The Hobbit*, to the wheedling, clever, cowardly Chrysophylax the Rich of "Farmer Giles of Ham," a humorous short story set not in the fantasy realm of Middle-earth but rather in an imagined medieval England. It should be no surprise to find that Tolkien himself admitted that when he was a child, he "desired dragons with a profound desire."[cviii]

Although all of Tolkien's dragons are worthy of further discussion, I will concentrate on the parallels between Fafnir in the *Saga of the Volsungs*, on the one hand, and Smaug and Glaurung in Tolkien's books *The Hobbit* and *The Silmarillion*, respectively, on the other. Bilbo's interaction with Smaug in *The Hobbit* also has resonances with the Anglo-Saxon epic poem *Beowulf*, and there are two small points of resemblance between Glaurung in *The Silmarillion* and the unnamed dragon in the *Saga of Ragnar Lothbrok*.

Author Jonathan Evans notes some parallels between Smaug, the dragon in *The Hobbit*, and the dragon in the last part of *Beowulf* in the events that trigger their rampages. In both stories, the dragons become enraged over the loss of one small cup from each of their hoards.[cix] Bilbo takes the cup in *The Hobbit* during his first visit to Smaug's lair, while in *Beowulf* the item is stolen by a man who goes unnamed.[cx]

The manner of Smaug's death comes from a different source, instead echoing Sigurd's slaying of the dragon Fafnir in the *Saga of the Volsungs*. In both stories, the dragon is brought low by a weapon piercing a weak spot in the underbelly near the left shoulder. Fafnir dies from a sword thrust given by Sigurd, who hides in a pit and attacks the dragon as he passes overhead, while Smaug is killed by an arrow shot by a Lakeman named Bard.[cxi]

In each case, the person killing the dragon is given advice on how to go about it. In *Volsungs*, Sigurd's foster-father, Regin, tells Sigurd to dig and hide in a pit and to stab the dragon as it passes overhead. As Sigurd is digging, Odin, appearing in the guise of an old, one-eyed man, tells Sigurd to dig multiple pits to protect himself from being overwhelmed by the flow of the dragon's blood. In *The Hobbit*, a thrush that has been hanging around the dwarves' camp overhears Bilbo telling the dwarves about the weakness he observed when he first entered the dragon's lair.[cxii] The thrush then carries this information to the Lakeman Bard.[cxiii] Bard's ability to understand the speech of birds also recalls *Volsungs*: Sigurd gains that same ability when he accidentally tastes some of Fafnir's blood after killing him, and the birds' speech to one another saves Sigurd's life just as the thrush saves Bard's, by warning Sigurd that his foster-father, Regin, intends to kill him.[cxiv]

As in *The Hobbit*, Tolkien appropriates some details from Sigurd's story in the *Saga of the Volsungs* for reuse in the story of Turin Turambar in *The Silmarillion*. Some of these are small elements: for example, both Turin and Sigurd wear dragon-helms and wield twice-forged swords, and both suffer unhappy fates. Here, however, I would like to concentrate on each hero's interactions with the dragons they slay. For Sigurd, this is Fafnir, while for Turin, this is Glaurung, the first dragon created in Middle-earth through the power of Morgoth, the Dark Lord.

As we have seen, Sigurd slays Fafnir with a sword thrust from below. Turin does the same in his final encounter with Glaurung but with rather more risk to Turin, who instead of waiting in relative safety inside a pit, climbs a cliff on one side of a chasm to await the dragon as it passes over the gap between the place where Turin waits and the other side.

The final scene including both Turin and Glaurung also has some resonances with the *Saga of Ragnar Lothbrok*. Ragnar gains the nickname "Lothbrok," or "shaggy breeches," because of the suit he makes to protect himself from the venom and blood of the dragon. The suit is effective: when some of the dying dragon's blood splashes on Ragnar, he is unhurt. Turin, on the other hand, is not as lucky or perhaps not as foresighted as Ragnar. When Turin pulls his sword out of Glaurung's side, the dragon's blood gushes out, and some lands on Turin's hand, burning it. And like the dragon in Ragnar's story, Glaurung has no wings.

The characters of Fafnir, Smaug, and Glaurung themselves also have some things in common, especially in the ways in which they relate to Sigurd, Bilbo, and Turin, respectively. Tolkien takes these commonalities and molds them somewhat differently for Smaug than he does for Glaurung, partly because of the tone of each of these stories. The story of Turin Turambar is both a tragedy and also a romance in the medieval sense of the word, having been written in a deliberately archaic voice intended to evoke the sense that what one is reading is a document from an ancient past, not something created by a twentieth-century Oxford don. *The Hobbit,* by contrast, for all its battles, giant spiders, goblins, and dragons, was written for children and so maintains a fairly lighthearted tone.

Unlike the dragon in Ragnar's saga, who remains silent throughout his encounter with Ragnar, Fafnir and Tolkien's dragons speak to the heroes of their respective stories. After Sigurd gives Fafnir his death blow, Fafnir asks, "Who is thy father, and what thy race?" Sigurd answers, "My race is unknown to men; I am called the Noble Beast, and I have no father or mother, for I have journeyed alone."[cxv] In the conversation that follows, Sigurd reveals his true name and endures a series of slights by the dragon followed by an exchange about death and fate before Fafnir curses his treasure and then dies.

In this conversation, Sigurd and Fafnir relate to one another more or less as equals. They ask and answer one another's questions, and although Fafnir tries to frighten Sigurd with dire portents to follow if Sigurd touches Fafnir's treasure, the dragon does not seem to think of Sigurd as being somehow beneath him.

Glaurung, by contrast, is openly contemptuous of Turin. The dragon insults Turin, much as Fafnir does Sigurd, but Glaurung's taunts are significantly more venomous. At their first meeting, Glaurung does not kill Turin; he instead wounds the hero psychologically and emotionally by calling him "[t]hankless fosterling, outlaw, slayer of thy friend, thief of love, usurper of Nargothrond, captain foolhardy and deserter of thy kin."[cxvi] Now, all of these things are technically true and are descriptions of actual events from Turin's life, but Glaurung is using them and the insults against Turin's family that follow to make Turin doubt himself and thus weaken him in the fight against Glaurung's creator, Morgoth. Although Turin then attempts to attack Glaurung, the dragon simply dodges out of the way and then slithers off while making further taunts, apparently thinking he has already wasted too much time and effort on this puny man who is beneath his notice.[cxvii]

Another exchange takes place later in the story, this time between Glaurung and Nienor, Turin's wife, as Glaurung is dying. Glaurung mocks Nienor with the news that she is actually Turin's sister—a fact of which neither Nienor nor Turin were aware—after which Glaurung denigrates Turin yet again before dying.[cxviii] Not long afterward, Turin learns that his mother has died and that Nienor has lost her memory and run away.[cxix] Exhausted and bereft, Turin kills himself by throwing himself onto the blade of his sword.[cxx]

Tolkien takes Sigurd's interaction with Fafnir and uses it as the model for Glaurung's conversations with Turin and Nienor but expands on his model by creating three encounters instead of one involving not one but two characters. Tolkien also heightens the emotional stakes by making Glaurung's speeches to Turin and Nienor even more cruel than Fafnir's to Sigurd, as well as by elevating the dragon's malice toward the humans he torments.

In *The Hobbit*, by contrast, Tolkien instead takes the riddling part of Sigurd's conversation with Fafnir as the model for Bilbo's interaction with Smaug, increasing the number of riddles and using the conversation as an opportunity for Smaug to gloat over his superiority to the puny thief who dares confront him and touch even the smallest item of his treasure. Unlike Glaurung's gloating and taunts, which become the undoing both of Turin and of Nienor, Smaug's insults hold the seeds of his own destruction: he boasts about his gem-encrusted underbelly and then shows it to Bilbo, who spies the one bald patch on the left side that will become the dragon's bane. Further, Bilbo's more or less successful riddling shows the courage and sharp wits of the little Hobbit who, only a few months earlier, was "kneeling on the hearth-rug, shaking like a jelly that was melting" at the suggestion he would be going on a serious adventure with Gandalf and the Dwarves.[cxxi] Unlike Turin, Bilbo comes away emboldened from his encounter with a dragon.

Like Bilbo, Sigurd begins his interaction with Fafnir by concealing his identity within a series of riddles, but Sigurd quickly gives up the pretense when Fafnir insists he tell the truth. Sigurd does, not least because he knows the dragon is dying and won't be able to come after him later. Bilbo, however, has no such assurances since Smaug is very much alive, and there is no guarantee that he will be destroyed. Also, while Sigurd treats Fafnir more or less as a defeated peer, Bilbo, by contrast, realizes how very small and powerless he is—with which Smaug obviously agrees—and so addresses the dragon by flattering titles such as "Smaug the Tremendous" and "Smaug the Chiefest and Greatest of Calamities."[cxxii]

When Smaug asks who Bilbo is and where he comes from, Bilbo replies with a series of riddles that refer obliquely both to his origins and to the adventures he has had up to this point:

I come from under the hill, and under the hills and over the hills my paths led. And through the air. I am he that walks unseen.... I am the clue-finder, the web-cutter, the stinging fly. I was chosen for the lucky number.... I am he that buries his friends alive and drowns them and draws them alive again from the water. I came from the end of a bag, but no bag went over me.... I am the friend of bears and the guest of eagles. I am Ringwinner and Luckwearer; and I am Barrel-rider.[cxxiii]

After this bit of dialogue, Tolkien goes on to give the reader some instruction in interacting with dragons, noting that it is wise to hide one's name but unwise to refuse to answer at all, and that therefore Bilbo is doing very well indeed in this extraordinarily dangerous situation. Tolkien then explains why it is a good idea to approach dragons this way, saying that "[n]o dragon can resist the fascination of riddling talk and of wasting time trying to understand it."[cxxiv]

This is true of Fafnir just as it is true of Smaug: as Fafnir is dying, he tries to work out the riddle of Sigurd's identity, which is then followed by a series of questions and answers about the nature of the Norns, the goddesses who determine the fates of all human beings, and the dwelling place of the fire god Surt, before Fafnir goes on to warn Sigurd about the doom that will be upon him if he touches Fafnir's gold.[cxxv]

In his own fiction, Tolkien took the Norse stories he so deeply loved and which he knew so intimately and used them as inspiration for new characters and events. But instead of copying what he found in the sagas, Tolkien reworked them, adapting them to his own ends and making them rich elements on which to base fresh stories, stories for readers who, like Tolkien, desire dragons with a profound desire.

Notes to "Dragons in Tolkien's Middle-Earth"

Kirsten Wolf, *Daily Life of the Vikings* (Westport: The Greenwood Press, 2004), p. 22.

[1] Wolf, *Daily Life*, p. 22.

[1] Wolf, *Daily Life*, p. 22.

[1] Richard Hall, *The World of the Vikings* (New York: Thames and Hudson, 2007), pp. 40-43.

[1] Anders Winroth, *The Age of the Vikings* (Princeton: Princeton University Press, 2014), pp. 138-9.

[1] James Graham-Campbell, ed., *Cultural Atlas of the Viking World* (Oxford: Andromeda, 1994), p. 63.

[1] Graham-Campbell, *Cultural Atlas*, pp. 80-83.

[1] Wolf, *Daily Life*, p. 8.

[1] Wolf, *Daily Life*, pp. 10-11.

[1] Wolf, *Daily Life*, pp. 22-24.

[1] Winroth, *Age of the Vikings*, pp. 164-65.

[1] The stories of women warriors in Saxo's history are summarized in Judith Jesch, *Women in the Viking Age* (Woodbridge: The Boydell Press, 1991), pp. 176ff.

[1] Charlotte Hendenstierna-Jonson et al., "A Female Viking Warrior Confirmed by Genomics," *American Journal of Physical Anthropology* 164/4 (2017): 853-60.

[1] Hendenstierna-Jonson et al., "Female Viking Warrior," p. 855.

[1] Hendenstierna-Jonson et al., "Female Viking Warrior," p. 855-57.

[1] Hall, *World of the Vikings*, p. 34.

[1] Jesch, *Women in the Viking Age*, pp. 183-85.

[1] Wolf, *Daily Life*, p. 13.

[1] Wolf, *Daily Life*, pp. 8-9.

[1] Wolf, *Daily Life*, p. 10.

[1] Wolf, *Daily Life*, p. 10.

[1] Winroth, *Age of the Vikings*, pp. 162-64.

[1] Winroth, *Age of the Vikings*, pp. 162-64.

[1] Winroth, *Age of the Vikings*, pp. 163-64.

[1] Neil Oliver, *The Vikings: A New History* (New York: Pegasus Books LLC, 2013), p. 108.

[1] Winroth, *Age of the Vikings*, p. 123.

[1] John Haywood, *Northmen: The Viking Saga AD 793-1241* (New York: St. Martin's Press, 2015), p. 14.

[1] Wolf, *Daily Life*, p. 24; Graham-Campbell, *Cultural Atlas*, p. 75.

[1] Haywood, *Northmen*, pp. 20-22; Graham-Campell, *Cultural Atlas*, p. 75.

[1] Haywood, *Northmen*, p. 22.

[1] Graham-Campbell, *Cultural Atlas*, p. 75.

[1] Graham-Campbell, *Cultural Atlas*, p. 79.

[1] Wolf, *Daily Life*, p. 24.

[1] Graham-Campbell, *Cultural Atlas*, p. 78.

[1] Graham-Campbell, *Cultural Atlas*, p. 78.

[1] Hall, *World of the Vikings*, pp. 33, 99.

[1] Hall, *World of the Vikings*, p. 101.

[1] Hall, *World of the Vikings*, p. 101.

[1] Winroth, *Age of the Vikings*, pp. 124-27,

[1] Graham-Campbell, *Cultural Atlas*, p. 78.

[1] Graham-Campbell, *Cultural Atlas*, p. 85.

[1] Hall, *World of the Vikings*, p. 59.

[1] Hall, *World of the Vikings*, p. 60.

[1] Hall, *World of the Vikings*, p. 60. Ribe is a town in Denmark.
[1] Haywood, *Northmen*, pp. 42-3.
[1] Haywood, *Northmen*, p. 45.
[1] Haywood, *Northmen*, pp. 45, 88.
[1] Haywood, *Northmen*, pp. 169-70.
[1] Haywood, *Northmen*, p. 40.
[1] Winroth, *Age of the Vikings*, p. 136.
[1] Winroth, *Age of the Vikings*, pp. 136-39.
[1] Winroth, *Age of the Vikings*, pp. 136-37.
[1] Oliver, *New History*, pp. 99-100.
[1] Hall, *Vikings*, p. 54.
[1] Winroth, *Age of the Vikings*, p. 75.
[1] Haywood, *Northmen*, p. 47.
[1] Haywood, *Northmen*, p. 50.
[1] Oliver, New History, p. 169.
[1] Caroline Taggart, *The Book of English Place Names: How Our Towns and Villages Got Their Names* (n. p.: Ebury Press, 2011), pp. 15, 82, 269.
[1] Graham-Campbell, *Cultural Atlas*, pp. 190-91; Winroth, *Age of the Vikings*, p. 114.
[1] Graham-Campbell, *Cultural Atlas*, pp. 190-91.
[1] Graham-Campbell, *Cultural Atlas*, p. 192; Hall, *Vikings*, p. 97.
[1] Hall, *Vikings*, pp. 150, 152.
[1] Hall, *Vikings*, p. 151.
[1] Hall, *Vikings*, p. 181.
[1] Hall, *Vikings*, p. 160.
[1] Hall, *Vikings*, p. 161.
[1] Ben Waggoner, trans., *The Sagas of Ragnar Lodbrok* (New Haven: The Troth, 2009), p. xiii.
[1] Waggoner, *Sagas of Ragnar Lodbrok*, p. xi.
[1] Waggoner, *Sagas of Ragnar Lodbrok*, p. xiii.
[1] Waggoner, *Sagas of Ragnar Lodbrok*, p. xxiv. The manuscript in question is Copenhagen, Royal Danish Library, MS NkS 1824b 4to.

[1] This manuscript is Copenhagen, Royal Danish Library, MS AM 147 4to. Waggoner, *Sagas of Ragnar Lodbrok*, p. xxiv.

[1] Waggoner, *Sagas of Ragnar Lodbrok*, p. xxv. Waggoner also notes that the *Hauksbók* was broken up into its constituent pieces, and the pieces were rebound and catalogued separately. The portion containing the *Tale of Ragnar's Sons* now resides in the Arnamagnaean Institute at the University of Copenhagan as MS AM 544.

[1] Robert Crawford, *Scotland's Books: A History of Scottish Literature* (Oxford: Oxford University Press, 2009), n. p., accessed through Google Books <http://google.com/books> 23 March 2020.

[1] n. a., "Teutonic Forms," p. 3 (PDF accessed via https://www.jsicmail.ac.uk, 23 March 2020). The PDF appears to cite Turville-Petre, p. xix, as a source for the definition of *háttlausa* but does not give a bibliographical description beyond the author's surname and page number. It is possible that this information was taken from *Scaldic Poetry* by Gabriel Turville-Petre (Oxford: Clarendon Press, 1976), p. xxix, but I do not have access to this volume and so cannot confirm the accuracy of this assumption.

[1] Waggoner, *Sagas of Ragnar Lodbrok*, p. x.

[1] Oliver Elton, trans. *The Nine Books of the Danish History of Saxo Grammaticus*. 2 vols. (London: Norroena Society, [1905]).

[1] Elton, trans., *Saxo Grammaticus*, vol. 2, pp. 544-5.

[1] Elton, trans., *Saxo Grammaticus*, vol. 2, pp. 550 (Charlemagne episode) and 552-4 (Hellespont episode).

[1] Winroth, *Age of the Vikings*, pp. 134-38.

[1] Wolf, *Daily Life*, p. 55.

[1] Wolf, *Daily Life*, p. 55.

[1] Crawford, *Volsungs*, p. xv.

[1] R. Bartlett, "The Viking Hiatus in the Cult of Saints as Seen in the Twelfth Century," in *The Long Twelfth-Century View of the Anglo-Saxon Past*, edited by Martin Brett and David A. Woodman (Abingdon: Routledge, 2016), p. 18. Bartlett cites the F manuscript of the *Chronicle*, f. 54. "Viking Hiatus," n. 16.

[1] Bartlett, "Viking Hiatus," pp. 17-8.

[1] Bartlett, "Viking Hiatus," p. 18.

[1] Waggoner, *Sagas of Ragnar Lodbrok*, pp. xvi-xvii.

[1] Crawford, *Volsungs*, p. xix.

[1] Albert Welles, *The Pedigree and History of the Washington Family* (New York: Society Library, 1879).

[1] Welles, *Washington*, p. iv.

[1] In one medieval version of the saga, Ragnar states that he is fifteen years old in his verse to Thora, but this version does not include Ragnar's sojourn with Lagertha. Because I am including the story about Ragnar meeting and marrying Lagertha prior to his encounter with the dragon, I have changed Ragnar's age to eighteen to take his three years with Lagertha into account.

[1] A kenning for "dragon."

[1] Another kenning for "dragon."

[1] A kenning for "black." This is also a play on the name "Kraka," which itself means "crow."

[1] The original sources are unclear about what the exact nature of Ivar's disability was. In some ways, the descriptions seem to suggest a milder form of brittle bone disease (*osteogenesis imperfecta*), but they could also refer to rickets. Rickets is a childhood ailment that leads to a softening of the bones, which is caused by a lack of vitamin D. Effects of this softening include bow-leggedness and knock knees, which impairs one's ability to walk. Rickets is more common in northern latitudes because of the lack of sunlight during a significant part of the year. It can also be caused by genetic factors or by the mother having a severe vitamin D deficiency during pregnancy.

[1] Kraka/Aslaug's father also had the ability to understand the speech of birds, which he acquired by accidentally tasting some of the dragon Fafnir's blood while roasting its heart for Regin, the blacksmith to whom Sigurd was apprenticed and who was the brother of Fafnir.

[1] "Fafnirsbane" means "Killer of Fafnir."

[1] Although the saga was only written down in Christian times, one wonders whether the pit of snakes was intended to be some kind of reference to the pagan concept either of Hvergelmir or of Nastrandir. The latter was a place in the Norse underworld that was made out of venomous serpents, and the former was a place inhabited by a giant serpent. Nastrandir was the place to which the souls of oathbreakers and murderers were consigned and Hvergelmir the place where the souls of the most wicked were consumed by the giant serpent. If this coincidence of imagery between pagan beliefs and the saga's text were in fact intended, it may add yet more degradation to the method used for Ragnar's death since it signals that Ella finds him to be not a noble enemy but rather a dishonorable murderer. It is also possible that a link was intended to be made between Ragnar and Gunnar from the *Saga of the Volsungs*, who also meets his end in a pit of snakes.

¹ This is a significantly shortened version of the *Krákumál*, a 29-stave poem purported to be Ragnar's death-song. In fact, the *Krákumál* is a twelfth-century creation, probably written somewhere in the Scottish islands.

¹ Payment of wergild was an important practice in ancient Germanic and Scandinavian societies. The purpose of wergild was to compensate a victim—or the victim's family, if the victim had been killed—for the hurt they had received through the perpetrator's commission of a crime. The amount to be paid varied depending on the nature of the injury and the gender and social status of the parties concerned. Once wergild had been paid, the victim and/or their family had to relinquish any right to exact further payment or vengeance.

¹ Some of the sources I consulted said that "Lundunaborg" was London; others said that it was Lincoln. Neither identification can be historically accurate since both London and Lincoln were founded by the Romans long before the Vikings ever arrived in England. Peter Munch is in the "London" camp in his *Norse Mythology: Legends of Gods and Heroes* (New York: American-Scandinavian Foundation, 1926), p. 251. Katharine F. Boult, on the other hand, claims that Ivar's stronghold was Lincoln. *Asgard & the Norse Heroes* (London: J. M. Dent & Sons, Ltd., [1914]), p. 253.

¹ The medieval sources do not agree on exactly what Ella's torture and death entailed. Some seem to indicate that the image of an eagle was carved into his back, but another version states that the "eagle" was created by cracking open the victim's rib cage from the back and then splaying his lungs out as though they were wings. Historian Anders Winroth says that the difficulty in translating the original Old Norse has led to other misunderstandings of the "blood eagle." Winroth says that the interpretation in which an eagle is carved into Ella's back with a knife likewise may be a mistranslation, although he finds it grammatically correct, and that it might have been the saga creator's original intent to say that Ella was killed and then his body left as food for birds of prey. *The Age of the Vikings* (Princeton: Princeton University Press, 2014), pp. 36-7.

¹ Quoted in Henry Resnick, "The Hobbit-Forming World of J. R. R. Tolkien," *The Saturday Evening Post* (2 July 1966), p. 94. Tolkien was less sanguine about the Celtic influences on his work and was offended when an early reviewer of *The Silmarillion* said they noticed a Celtic influence. Marjorie J. Burns, *Perilous Realms: Celtic and Norse in Tolkien's Middle-earth* (Toronto: University of Toronto Press, 2005), n.p., accessed via Google Books, 18 March 2020 <http://www.google.com/books>.

¹ Humphrey Carpenter, *Tolkien: A Biography* (Boston: Houghton Mifflin Company, 1977), pp. 22, 35-36.

¹ Carpenter, *Tolkien,* p. 34-5.

[1] Carpenter, *Tolkien*, p. 71.

[1] Carpenter, *Tolkien*, pp. 111, 200.

[1] J. R. R. Tolkien, "On Fairy-Stories," in *Essays Presented to Charles Williams* (London: Oxford University Press, 1947), p. 64.

[1] Jonathan Evans, "The Dragon-Lore of Middle Earth: Tolkien and Old English and Old Norse Tradition," in *J. R. R. Tolkien and His Literary Resonances: Views of Middle Earth*, ed. George Clark and Daniel Timmons (Westport: Greenwood Press, 2000), 21-38.

[1] Evans, "Dragon-Lore," p. 31.

[1] Margaret Schlauch, trans., *The Saga of the Volsungs: The Saga of Ragnar Lodbrok Together with the Lay of Kraka* (New York: The American Scandinavian Foundation, 1930), p. 96; J. R. R. Tolkien, *The Hobbit* (Boston: Houghton Mifflin Company, 1966), p. 262.

[1] Schlauch, *Volsungs*, p. 95; Tolkien, *Hobbit*, p. 240.

[1] Tolkien, *Hobbit*, p. 261.

[1] Schlauch, *Volsungs*, p. 101.

[1] Schlauch, *Volsungs*, pp. 96-7.

[1] J. R. R. Tolkien, *The Silmarillion*, ed. Christopher Tolkien (Boston: Houghton Mifflin Company, 1977), p. 213-14.

[1] Tolkien, *Silmarillion*, p. 214

[1] Tolkien, *Silmarillion*, p. 223.

[1] Tolkien, *Silmarillion*, p. 225.

[1] Tolkien, *Silmarillion*, p. 225.

[1] Tolkien, *Hobbit*, p. 25.

[1] Tolkien, *Hobbit*, p. 234.

[1] Tolkien, *Hobbit*. p. 235.

[1] Tolkien, *Hobbit*, p. 235.

[1] Schlauch, *Volsungs*, p. 96-9.

The Clash of History and Drama in the History Channel Television Series *Vikings*

The television series *Vikings*, written and produced by Michael Hirst, ran for six seasons and 79 episodes between 2013 and 2019. As of this writing, a ten-episode extension of season six is planned to be released in 2020. Grounded in a great deal of historical research, the series follows the life and deeds of Ragnar Lothbrok (Travis Fimmel), his wife Lagertha (Katheryn Winnick), his brother Rollo (Clive Standen), and other Viking characters living in the Scandinavian village of Kattegat in the late eighth century.

    The series has garnered praise for its high production values and strong writing,[cxxvi] but it has also been subject to criticism for its many historical inaccuracies, which likely arise, at least in part, from the screenwriters' need to structure the episodes and the seasons according to the demands of the television drama genre.[cxxvii] The interactions among historicity, historical inaccuracy, newly created fiction, and the text of the *Saga of Ragnar Lothbrok* in *Vikings* is well worth exploring. However, I do not propose to analyze the entire series here; instead, I will focus on just a few points from the first season that demonstrate these kinds of rich interactions.

The underlying inspiration for *Vikings* was the *Saga of Ragnar Lothbrok* and its continuation in the *Tale of Ragnar's Sons*, along with the history of the early Viking Age. Although the series does incorporate some of the details and characters from the saga, it does not follow the saga's plot with any faithfulness. Instead, Ragnar's saga and actual Viking history provide something of a basic framework on which to scaffold the series. This was done in accordance with Hirst's desire to create a viable drama "based on historical research and historical record," not with making a documentary or with directly adapting Ragnar's saga.[cxxviii] Hirst therefore twists and remolds both the saga and Viking history to allow the Ragnar of the series to partake in events that would have happened long before the historical Ragnar's birth and to interact with other persons, both historical and newly fabricated, who either have no connection to the saga or who exist within the saga but have different interactions with Ragnar and some of the other characters.

There are several reasons why it was more fruitful for Hirst to borrow the idea of Ragnar from the saga but not reproduce the saga itself. One has to do with duration: the original saga would not give the creators of the show as much material to work with as creating a new story using the saga as a springboard. Another has to do with the desire for a modicum of historicity: although we might associate the Viking Age with things like dragons, dragons have never existed. Nor have magical cows that frighten away an army of warriors, for that matter. There is a limit to the degree to which one might have a historically informed series and at the same time reproduce the *Saga of Ragnar Lothbrok* as it stands.

However, a more important reason for incorporating plot elements and characters that are ahistorical has to do with story structure and audience expectations. The *Saga of Ragnar Lothbrok*, like most tales of its sort, has an episodic structure, wherein the story is made up of a series of connected scenes, or episodes, that move us from one end of the story to the other. In the case of the *Saga of Ragnar Lothbrok*, these episodes are made of events from Ragnar's life that move him from the point at which he becomes king after the death of his father, through his marriage to Lagertha, to slaying the dragon, and so on, to the end when he is executed at the hands of King Ella. Episodic structure is one valid way of telling a story, but it is not how most modern visual entertainment is composed.

Modern dramas usually have a three-act dramatic structure, which is the format that Western audiences expect from films and television since they believe it to give a satisfying shape to the story being told. In dramatic structure, the first act introduces the protagonist and shows an inciting event that requires the protagonist to do something by introducing a problem that must be solved. The second act contains the "meat" of the story, where the main conflict and any subsidiary conflicts are played out between the protagonist and the other characters. From the inciting event through act 2 and into act 3, the structural principle of rising tension requires the stakes, the action, and the conflict to continue to increase until the final battle (which may or may not involve actual physical combat, depending on the story being told) in act 3.

Once the main conflict of the drama has been resolved, what remains is the denouement (which literally means "untying"), where the story is brought to a close. In the case of an ongoing series that has a larger dramatic arc, the denouement of one episode—from this point onward referring to one broadcast unit of the series—might function as both an ending for that episode itself and a springboard to the next. Episodes that end on cliffhangers lack a denouement entirely since the cliffhanger suspends the story in the middle of the action, leaving the denouement to the episode that concludes the story as a whole.

Some of the historical inaccuracies and departures from the medieval *Saga of Ragnar Lothbrok* in *Vikings* likely are the result of the screenwriters wishing to adhere to the principles underlying dramatic structure, which requires conflict between a clearly defined protagonist and a clearly defined antagonist who move through the story participating in action that conforms to the principle of rising tension. The screenwriters also need to follow the principle referred to as "show, don't tell," wherein important exposition is delivered in ways other than by having the characters' dialogue or a voiceover explain things to the audience. Although "show, don't tell" is also a principle for written things like novels, it is especially important for film and television, which are both visual media.

In the first season of *Vikings*, Ragnar—who here is a farmer and family man living in the village of Kattegat, not the son of a king as in the saga—is working together with his friend, the eccentric shipwright Floki (Gustaf Skarsgård), to create a new kind of ship that will be able to sail the North Atlantic and survive bad weather. Ragnar intends to sail westward to see what he can find because he's tired of going on raids to the east. However, Earl Haraldson (Gabriel Byrne), the local nobleman who holds sway over Kattegat, doesn't want Ragnar to go on this voyage. Haraldson is jealous of Ragnar's enterprising spirit because he sees Ragnar as competition for the loyalties of the men under his jurisdiction.

Ragnar disobeys the earl's direct order not to sail west. Ragnar and Floki, along with Ragnar's brother, Rollo, and other men, sail in Floki's new ship to England. On the journey, they contend with a great storm that might have destroyed other ships, but they weather the storm successfully. Floki is elated that his design works as intended. The Vikings beach their ship on the holy island of Lindisfarne off the coast of England. There they go ashore and raid Lindisfarne's monastery, killing some of the monks and taking others captive as slaves. Among the captives is Athelstan (George Blagden), a young English monk who becomes Ragnar's slave and then his friend.

Although the raid and the trial of Floki's ship design are both successful, all is not well. When the Vikings return home, Earl Haraldson is angry that Ragnar disobeyed him, so he confiscates the treasure that Ragnar and his friends looted from the monastery. The conflict between the earl and Ragnar then drives the arc for the rest of the season, running in parallel both with an important secondary conflict between Ragnar and his brother, Rollo, who is jealous of his brother's leadership, and also with the developing relationship between Ragnar and Athelstan.

In this very brief synopsis of the first two episodes of the first season, we can already see several historical inaccuracies—some of them quite glaring—as well as several departures from the text of the original saga. The first set of inaccuracies concerns elements of Ragnar's forbidden raid. Specifically, these are the idea that Britain was *terra nova* to the Vikings, the idea that the Vikings did not already have ships capable of sailing the North Atlantic even in storms, and the conflict between the date of the actual historical raid on Lindisfarne and the life of the historical Ragnar or Ragnars mentioned in contemporary chronicles.

The historical raid on Lindisfarne happened in 793, while the man or composite character who became the protagonist of the *Saga of Ragnar Lothbrok* was active in the middle of the ninth century. The historical Ragnar likely had not even been born when Lindisfarne was raided, and neither the medieval chronicles nor Ragnar's saga mention any trip to England other than Ragnar's final, fatal attack on Northumbria. It also seems unlikely either that Viking shipbuilding technology was incapable of weathering the North Atlantic until the point at which Lindisfarne was raided or that the Vikings did not already know something about what lay to the west of their native shores before that point.

By incorporating these three concepts into the first part of *Vikings*, Hirst is creating important stakes for Ragnar and the other characters. One raising of the stakes is Ragnar's sailing in an untested ship to unknown lands, which is much more exciting than using technology that is already familiar to sail to a place everyone already knows about. Hirst also uses Ragnar's plans to sail west on a voyage of exploration and plunder in order to introduce the relationship between Ragnar and Floki, which at first centers around the new ship design, and also on the relationship between Ragnar and Rollo, which will be a source of continuing conflict for much of the series that follows. Not only that, but latching onto the famous raid on Lindisfarne puts the fictional raid of *Vikings'* Ragnar on the historical map, as it were, by placing the main character into the center of events that are historically significant and relatively well known. This has the effect of raising the status of the protagonist with respect to this particular element of his adventure.

In addition to twisting historical events to his own ends, Hirst also manipulates historical characters, primarily Ragnar, but also others. For example, a Viking named Rollo did, in fact, exist, although he was of no relation to Ragnar. This Rollo is thought to have participated in the Viking siege of Paris in 885, an event that Hirst also incorporated into his television series beginning in season 3. The historical Rollo was not active only in that one siege; in fact, by 885, he had already been a scourge of northern France for almost a decade, having set up a base in Rouen around 876.[cxxix] Rollo went on to conduct many raids until he finally was defeated in 911 when he attempted to take Chartres. A peace deal with the French king gave Rollo control over the area around Rouen in exchange for the cessation of raids and Rollo's conversion to Christianity.[cxxx] Hirst's Rollo also converts to Christianity as part of a peace deal, but this happens in connection with another raid on England in the season 1 episode "A King's Ransom."

By bringing Rollo into the world of *Vikings*, Hirst creates an important point of conflict for Ragnar. Hirst's Rollo has an uneasy relationship with his brother, teetering between working with him as an ally and working against him as an enemy. The question of whether Rollo will help or hinder (or even kill) Ragnar adds texture to the relationship between these two characters and increases the number of potential storylines and subplots available to the writer.

The final element to be examined is the character of Earl Haraldson and his relationship to Ragnar. Unlike either Ragnar or Rollo, the earl is neither based on a historical figure nor taken from the *Saga of Ragnar Lothbrok*. Instead, Haraldson is a completely fictitious character created by Hirst specifically for this series. Some commentators have found Haraldson's character to be one of the most problematic aspects of the series, not because he is made up out of whole cloth but because of the way he is portrayed and the way he interacts with Ragnar and the other people over whom he rules.

In his 2014 review of the series, George Sim Johnston of the *American Spectator* was especially outraged by the earl's character.[cxxxi] Among the faults found by Johnston was the use of a patronymic ("Haraldson") as though it were a surname or even given name, when in fact Vikings from this period are usually referred to by their given names; for example, Leif Eiriksson is referred to in historical literature as "Leif," not "Eiriksson." But more outrageous to Johnston was the earl's behavior toward Ragnar and the people of Kattegat because Haraldson "rules like a feudal lord, dominating the governing assembly (the 'Thing'), bullying and threatening everyone."[cxxxii]

As Johnston points out in his review, this behavior runs counter to what we know of Viking governance in this period. Feudal, authoritarian modes of governance were not employed until the end of the Viking Age and were motivated in part by the adoption of Christianity by Scandinavian nobles.[cxxxiii] At the beginning of this period, the chieftain's authority derived from his ability to convince warriors to join and follow him. Moreover, the warriors would not have seen the chieftain as being inherently superior to themselves in any way.[cxxxiv]

If Earl Haraldson had been an actual late eighth-century chieftain, he would not have thought to deny Ragnar the opportunity to raid Lindisfarne because Ragnar wouldn't have needed his permission to go in the first place. Nor would Haraldson have confiscated the loot Ragnar and his companions bring back; to do so would have spelled a quick end to an earl's chieftainship and likely to the earl himself, since taking away treasure he had not earned would have been insulting in the extreme. Further, when Ragnar speaks out against Haraldson having condemned a man to be beheaded, Haraldson later tells Ragnar that he has overstepped by speaking against him in public.

Johnston states that the handling of Haraldson's character is "an expression of the tropes to which lazy scriptwriters are prone. Every story has to be about some dynamic young person (who wants freedom) in conflict with a hidebound old conservative, who lives by oppression."[cxxxv] However, what is driving the trope of young explorer vs. old oppressor that is at work here is the need to have a clearly defined antagonist who stands in opposition to the protagonist as part of the basic structure of the work.

Johnston may be correct in assessing Hirst's work as "lazy" on this point since it might well have been possible for Hirst to create a strong foil for Ragnar without running so blatantly afoul of actual Viking philosophies of governance. However, Hirst declined to write his story that way, instead presenting the earl as having strong authority over Ragnar and the others in Kattegat, when in reality early Viking-Age governance was significantly more democratic. For example, at a historical Thing, all free men had the right to speak on whatever item of business was being discussed, and decisions were made by casting lots.[cxxxvi] Behavior such as Haraldson's never would have been tolerated by the real Ragnar or his contemporaries.

Although the many historical inaccuracies in the series may vex historians and reviewers, *Vikings* nevertheless remains a compelling drama that is well written, gorgeously filmed, and full of fine performances from a talented cast of actors. In *Vikings*, we see the embodiment of the Italian proverb "si non è vero, è ben trovato," which loosely translated means, "even if it's not true, it's a good story." *Vikings*, by and large, is not true, in many senses of the word, but like the *Saga of Ragnar Lothbrok* from which the television series takes its inspiration, it nevertheless is a story very well told indeed.

Notes to "The Clash of History and Drama in the History Channel Television Series *Vikings*"

Kirsten Wolf, *Daily Life of the Vikings* (Westport: The Greenwood Press, 2004), p. 22.

[1] Wolf, *Daily Life*, p. 22.

[1] Wolf, *Daily Life*, p. 22.

[1] Richard Hall, *The World of the Vikings* (New York: Thames and Hudson, 2007), pp. 40-43.

[1] Anders Winroth, *The Age of the Vikings* (Princeton: Princeton University Press, 2014), pp. 138-9.

[1] James Graham-Campbell, ed., *Cultural Atlas of the Viking World* (Oxford: Andromeda, 1994), p. 63.

[1] Graham-Campbell, *Cultural Atlas*, pp. 80-83.

[1] Wolf, *Daily Life*, p. 8.

[1] Wolf, *Daily Life*, pp. 10-11.

[1] Wolf, *Daily Life*, pp. 22-24.

[1] Winroth, *Age of the Vikings*, pp. 164-65.

[1] The stories of women warriors in Saxo's history are summarized in Judith Jesch, *Women in the Viking Age* (Woodbridge: The Boydell Press, 1991), pp. 176ff.

[1] Charlotte Hendenstierna-Jonson et al., "A Female Viking Warrior Confirmed by Genomics," *American Journal of Physical Anthropology* 164/4 (2017): 853-60.

[1] Hendenstierna-Jonson et al., "Female Viking Warrior," p. 855.

[1] Hendenstierna-Jonson et al., "Female Viking Warrior," p. 855-57.

[1] Hall, *World of the Vikings*, p. 34.

[1] Jesch, *Women in the Viking Age*, pp. 183-85.

[1] Wolf, *Daily Life*, p. 13.

[1] Wolf, *Daily Life*, pp. 8-9.

[1] Wolf, *Daily Life*, p. 10.

[1] Wolf, *Daily Life*, p. 10.

[1] Winroth, *Age of the Vikings*, pp. 162-64.

[1] Winroth, *Age of the Vikings*, pp. 162-64.

[1] Winroth, *Age of the Vikings*, pp. 163-64.

[1] Neil Oliver, *The Vikings: A New History* (New York: Pegasus Books LLC, 2013), p. 108.

[1] Winroth, *Age of the Vikings*, p. 123.

[1] John Haywood, *Northmen: The Viking Saga AD 793-1241* (New York: St. Martin's Press, 2015), p. 14.

[1] Wolf, *Daily Life*, p. 24; Graham-Campbell, *Cultural Atlas*, p. 75.

[1] Haywood, *Northmen*, pp. 20-22; Graham-Campell, *Cultural Atlas*, p. 75.

[1] Haywood, *Northmen*, p. 22.

[1] Graham-Campbell, *Cultural Atlas*, p. 75.

[1] Graham-Campbell, *Cultural Atlas*, p. 79.

[1] Wolf, *Daily Life*, p. 24.

[1] Graham-Campbell, *Cultural Atlas*, p. 78.

[1] Graham-Campbell, *Cultural Atlas*, p. 78.

[1] Hall, *World of the Vikings*, pp. 33, 99.

[1] Hall, *World of the Vikings*, p. 101.

[1] Hall, *World of the Vikings*, p. 101.

[1] Winroth, *Age of the Vikings*, pp. 124-27,

[1] Graham-Campbell, *Cultural Atlas*, p. 78.
[1] Graham-Campbell, *Cultural Atlas*, p. 85.
[1] Hall, *World of the Vikings*, p. 59.
[1] Hall, *World of the Vikings*, p. 60.
[1] Hall, *World of the Vikings*, p. 60. Ribe is a town in Denmark.
[1] Haywood, *Northmen*, pp. 42-3.
[1] Haywood, *Northmen*, p. 45.
[1] Haywood, *Northmen*, pp. 45, 88.
[1] Haywood, *Northmen*, pp. 169-70.
[1] Haywood, *Northmen*, p. 40.
[1] Winroth, *Age of the Vikings*, p. 136.
[1] Winroth, *Age of the Vikings*, pp. 136-39.
[1] Winroth, *Age of the Vikings*, pp. 136-37.
[1] Oliver, *New History*, pp. 99-100.
[1] Hall, *Vikings*, p. 54.
[1] Winroth, *Age of the Vikings*, p. 75.
[1] Haywood, *Northmen*, p. 47.
[1] Haywood, *Northmen*, p. 50.
[1] Oliver, New History, p. 169.
[1] Caroline Taggart, *The Book of English Place Names: How Our Towns and Villages Got Their Names* (n. p.: Ebury Press, 2011), pp. 15, 82, 269.
[1] Graham-Campbell, *Cultural Atlas*, pp. 190-91; Winroth, *Age of the Vikings*, p. 114.
[1] Graham-Campbell, *Cultural Atlas*, pp. 190-91.
[1] Graham-Campbell, *Cultural Atlas*, p. 192; Hall, *Vikings*, p. 97.
[1] Hall, *Vikings*, pp. 150, 152.
[1] Hall, *Vikings,* p. 151.
[1] Hall, *Vikings*, p. 181.
[1] Hall, *Vikings*, p. 160.
[1] Hall, *Vikings*, p. 161.
[1] Ben Waggoner, trans., *The Sagas of Ragnar Lodbrok* (New Haven: The Troth, 2009), p. xiii.

[1] Waggoner, *Sagas of Ragnar Lodbrok*, p. xi.

[1] Waggoner, *Sagas of Ragnar Lodbrok*, p. xiii.

[1] Waggoner, *Sagas of Ragnar Lodbrok*, p. xxiv. The manuscript in question is Copenhagen, Royal Danish Library, MS NkS 1824b 4to.

[1] This manuscript is Copenhagen, Royal Danish Library, MS AM 147 4to. Waggoner, *Sagas of Ragnar Lodbrok*, p. xxiv.

[1] Waggoner, *Sagas of Ragnar Lodbrok*, p. xxv. Waggoner also notes that the *Hauksbók* was broken up into its constituent pieces, and the pieces were rebound and catalogued separately. The portion containing the *Tale of Ragnar's Sons* now resides in the Arnamagnaean Institute at the University of Copenhagan as MS AM 544.

[1] Robert Crawford, *Scotland's Books: A History of Scottish Literature* (Oxford: Oxford University Press, 2009), n. p., accessed through Google Books <http://google.com/books> 23 March 2020.

[1] n. a., "Teutonic Forms," p. 3 (PDF accessed via https://www.jsicmail.ac.uk, 23 March 2020). The PDF appears to cite Turville-Petre, p. xix, as a source for the definition of *háttlausa* but does not give a bibliographical description beyond the author's surname and page number. It is possible that this information was taken from *Scaldic Poetry* by Gabriel Turville-Petre (Oxford: Clarendon Press, 1976), p. xxix, but I do not have access to this volume and so cannot confirm the accuracy of this assumption.

[1] Waggoner, *Sagas of Ragnar Lodbrok*, p. x.

[1] Oliver Elton, trans. *The Nine Books of the Danish History of Saxo Grammaticus*. 2 vols. (London: Norroena Society, [1905]).

[1] Elton, trans., *Saxo Grammaticus*, vol. 2, pp. 544-5.

[1] Elton, trans., *Saxo Grammaticus*, vol. 2, pp. 550 (Charlemagne episode) and 552-4 (Hellespont episode).

[1] Winroth, *Age of the Vikings*, pp. 134-38.

[1] Wolf, *Daily Life*, p. 55.

[1] Wolf, *Daily Life*, p. 55.

[1] Crawford, *Volsungs*, p. xv.

[1] R. Bartlett, "The Viking Hiatus in the Cult of Saints as Seen in the Twelfth Century," in *The Long Twelfth-Century View of the Anglo-Saxon Past*, edited by Martin Brett and David A. Woodman (Abingdon: Routledge, 2016), p. 18. Bartlett cites the F manuscript of the *Chronicle*, f. 54. "Viking Hiatus," n. 16.

[1] Bartlett, "Viking Hiatus," pp. 17-8.

[1] Bartlett, "Viking Hiatus," p. 18.

[1] Waggoner, *Sagas of Ragnar Lodbrok*, pp. xvi-xvii.

[1] Crawford, *Volsungs,* p. xix.

[1] Albert Welles, *The Pedigree and History of the Washington Family* (New York: Society Library, 1879).

[1] Welles, *Washington*, p. iv.

[1] In one medieval version of the saga, Ragnar states that he is fifteen years old in his verse to Thora, but this version does not include Ragnar's sojourn with Lagertha. Because I am including the story about Ragnar meeting and marrying Lagertha prior to his encounter with the dragon, I have changed Ragnar's age to eighteen to take his three years with Lagertha into account.

[1] A kenning for "dragon."

[1] Another kenning for "dragon."

[1] A kenning for "black." This is also a play on the name "Kraka," which itself means "crow."

[1] The original sources are unclear about what the exact nature of Ivar's disability was. In some ways, the descriptions seem to suggest a milder form of brittle bone disease (*osteogenesis imperfecta*), but they could also refer to rickets. Rickets is a childhood ailment that leads to a softening of the bones, which is caused by a lack of vitamin D. Effects of this softening include bow-leggedness and knock knees, which impairs one's ability to walk. Rickets is more common in northern latitudes because of the lack of sunlight during a significant part of the year. It can also be caused by genetic factors or by the mother having a severe vitamin D deficiency during pregnancy.

[1] Kraka/Aslaug's father also had the ability to understand the speech of birds, which he acquired by accidentally tasting some of the dragon Fafnir's blood while roasting its heart for Regin, the blacksmith to whom Sigurd was apprenticed and who was the brother of Fafnir.

[1] "Fafnirsbane" means "Killer of Fafnir."

[1] Although the saga was only written down in Christian times, one wonders whether the pit of snakes was intended to be some kind of reference to the pagan concept either of Hvergelmir or of Nastrandir. The latter was a place in the Norse underworld that was made out of venomous serpents, and the former was a place inhabited by a giant serpent. Nastrandir was the place to which the souls of oathbreakers and murderers were consigned and Hvergelmir the place where the souls of the most wicked were consumed by the giant serpent. If this coincidence of imagery between pagan beliefs and the saga's text were in fact intended, it may

add yet more degradation to the method used for Ragnar's death since it signals that Ella finds him to be not a noble enemy but rather a dishonorable murderer. It is also possible that a link was intended to be made between Ragnar and Gunnar from the *Saga of the Volsungs*, who also meets his end in a pit of snakes.

[1] This is a significantly shortened version of the *Krákumál*, a 29-stave poem purported to be Ragnar's death-song. In fact, the *Krákumál* is a twelfth-century creation, probably written somewhere in the Scottish islands.

[1] Payment of wergild was an important practice in ancient Germanic and Scandinavian societies. The purpose of wergild was to compensate a victim—or the victim's family, if the victim had been killed—for the hurt they had received through the perpetrator's commission of a crime. The amount to be paid varied depending on the nature of the injury and the gender and social status of the parties concerned. Once wergild had been paid, the victim and/or their family had to relinquish any right to exact further payment or vengeance.

[1] Some of the sources I consulted said that "Lundunaborg" was London; others said that it was Lincoln. Neither identification can be historically accurate since both London and Lincoln were founded by the Romans long before the Vikings ever arrived in England. Peter Munch is in the "London" camp in his *Norse Mythology: Legends of Gods and Heroes* (New York: American-Scandinavian Foundation, 1926), p. 251. Katharine F. Boult, on the other hand, claims that Ivar's stronghold was Lincoln. *Asgard & the Norse Heroes* (London: J. M. Dent & Sons, Ltd., [1914]), p. 253.

[1] The medieval sources do not agree on exactly what Ella's torture and death entailed. Some seem to indicate that the image of an eagle was carved into his back, but another version states that the "eagle" was created by cracking open the victim's rib cage from the back and then splaying his lungs out as though they were wings. Historian Anders Winroth says that the difficulty in translating the original Old Norse has led to other misunderstandings of the "blood eagle." Winroth says that the interpretation in which an eagle is carved into Ella's back with a knife likewise may be a mistranslation, although he finds it grammatically correct, and that it might have been the saga creator's original intent to say that Ella was killed and then his body left as food for birds of prey. *The Age of the Vikings* (Princeton: Princeton University Press, 2014), pp. 36-7.

[1] Quoted in Henry Resnick, "The Hobbit-Forming World of J. R. R. Tolkien," *The Saturday Evening Post* (2 July 1966), p. 94. Tolkien was less sanguine about the Celtic influences on his work and was offended when an early reviewer of *The Silmarillion* said they noticed a Celtic influence. Marjorie J. Burns, *Perilous Realms: Celtic and Norse in Tolkien's Middle-earth* (Toronto: University of

Toronto Press, 2005), n.p., accessed via Google Books, 18 March 2020 <http://www.google.com/books>.

[1] Humphrey Carpenter, *Tolkien: A Biography* (Boston: Houghton Mifflin Company, 1977), pp. 22, 35-36.

[1] Carpenter, *Tolkien*, p. 34-5.

[1] Carpenter, *Tolkien*, p. 71.

[1] Carpenter, *Tolkien*, pp. 111, 200.

[1] J. R. R. Tolkien, "On Fairy-Stories," in *Essays Presented to Charles Williams* (London: Oxford University Press, 1947), p. 64.

[1] Jonathan Evans, "The Dragon-Lore of Middle Earth: Tolkien and Old English and Old Norse Tradition," in *J. R. R. Tolkien and His Literary Resonances: Views of Middle Earth*, ed. George Clark and Daniel Timmons (Westport: Greenwood Press, 2000), 21-38.

[1] Evans, "Dragon-Lore," p. 31.

[1] Margaret Schlauch, trans., *The Saga of the Volsungs: The Saga of Ragnar Lodbrok Together with the Lay of Kraka* (New York: The American Scandinavian Foundation, 1930), p. 96; J. R. R. Tolkien, *The Hobbit* (Boston: Houghton Mifflin Company, 1966), p. 262.

[1] Schlauch, *Volsungs*, p. 95; Tolkien, *Hobbit*, p. 240.

[1] Tolkien, *Hobbit*, p. 261.

[1] Schlauch, *Volsungs*, p. 101.

[1] Schlauch, *Volsungs*, pp. 96-7.

[1] J. R. R. Tolkien, *The Silmarillion*, ed. Christopher Tolkien (Boston: Houghton Mifflin Company, 1977), p. 213-14.

[1] Tolkien, *Silmarillion*, p. 214

[1] Tolkien, *Silmarillion*, p. 223.

[1] Tolkien, *Silmarillion*, p. 225.

[1] Tolkien, *Silmarillion*, p. 225.

[1] Tolkien, *Hobbit*, p. 25.

[1] Tolkien, *Hobbit*, p. 234.

[1] Tolkien, *Hobbit*. p. 235.

[1] Tolkien, *Hobbit*, p. 235.

[1] Schlauch, *Volsungs*, p. 96-9.

[1] See, for example, Phelim O'Neill, "Vikings: Don't Dismiss This Show as Game of Thrones-Lite," *The Guardian* (23 May 2014), <https://www.theguardian.com/tv-and-radio/tvandradioblog/2014/may/23/vikings-review-history-channel-game-of-thrones>, accessed 9 Mar 2020.

[1] See, for example, George Sim Johnston, "The History Channel Gets *Vikings* Precisely Wrong," *The American Spectator* (12 March 2013), <https://spectator.org/33770_history-channel-gets-vikings-precisely-wrong/>, accessed 9 Mar 2020.

[1] Michael Hirst, "Foreword," in *The World of Vikings* by Justin Pollard (San Francisco, Chronicle Books, 2015), p. 5.

[1] John Haywood, *Northmen: The Viking Saga AD 793-1241* (New York: St. Martin's Press, 2015), p. 98.

[1] Haywood, *Northmen*, pp. 99-100.

[1] Johnston, "The History Channel."

[1] Johnston, "The History Channel."

[1] Anders Winroth, *The Age of the Vikings* (Princeton: Princeton University Press, 2014), p. 143.

[1] Winroth, *Age of the Vikings*, p. 136.

[1] Johnston, "The History Channel."

[1] James Graham-Campbell, ed., *Cultural Atlas of the Viking World* (Oxford: Andromeda, 1994), p. 43.

Appendix: The Tale of Sigurd and Brynhild

The Saga of the Volsungs *is the epic tale of several generations of a single family. It was first written down in the thirteenth century, but the story is considerably older. The complete tale is preserved in both the* Poetic Edda *and in another source under the title* Volsungasaga. *The* Prose Edda *also contains a summary of the story.*

The family whose history is related in this saga is named after Volsung, a hero who is descended from the Norse god Odin. The first part of the story tells the story of Volsung's forebears before launching into the tale of his own family and descendants.

Kraka/Aslaug, Ragnar's third wife, is the child of the Volsung Sigurd and the Valkyrie Brynhild. Kraka's/Aslaug's function within Ragnar's story is to elevate Ragnar's status as a hero by linking him to the Volsungs by marriage.

The synopsis below does not cover the complete Saga of the Volsungs. *Instead, it presents only the part having to do with Sigurd and Brynhild, which is the section relevant to Ragnar's saga.*

Sigurd is the son of the hero Sigmund, who in turn is the son of Volsung. Sigurd's foster-father is a smith named Regin, who is tasked with the boy's education. One day, Regin asks Sigurd about his father's treasure and who is guarding it. Sigurd tells Regin that his wealth is guarded by the king. On another day, Regin tells Sigurd to ask the king for a horse; Sigurd does this, and the king agrees to give him one of his own horses.

The next day, Sigurd is walking through the woods on his way to choose a horse when he comes upon an old man. The old man asks Sigurd where he is going. Sigurd tells him he is going to choose a horse and asks advice of the old man. The old man tells Sigurd to drive a herd of horses into a river that is nearby. (The story doesn't explain where the horses come from, but they evidently do not belong to the king.) Sigurd does so, and all the horses swim across except for one grey horse. The old man tells Sigurd to take that horse; he explains that it is descended from Sleipnir, Odin's own horse, and that it has not yet been ridden by anyone. Sigurd calls the horse Grani. The old man tells Sigurd to take good care of the horse so that in time it will become the best steed in the whole world. Then the man disappears; he was really the god Odin.

Sigurd goes back home, where Regin again asks him about his wealth, which Regin seems to think is being unfairly denied to Sigurd. Then Regin tells Sigurd that he knows how Sigurd can get a lot of treasure and fame. Regin suggests that Sigurd kill the dragon Fafnir and take his gold. Sigurd balks at this. Regin taunts him about it, but Sigurd reminds him that he is still very young and can't be expected to go after dragons, no matter his lineage. Regin backs down and offers to tell Sigurd the story of Fafnir, and Sigurd asks him to tell it.

Regin explains how his brother Otr could transform himself into an otter and often went fishing in a place where the dwarf Andvari dwelled in the shape of a pike. One day, Otr catches a salmon, and when he takes it onto the riverbank, he is killed by Loki. Loki skins Otr and brings the pelt to Otr's father, Hreidmar. Hreidmar demands wergild for the murder of his son. Loki goes back to the river and takes Andvari's gold to use as wergild for Otr's death. The treasure includes a beautiful gold ring, which will have an important role to play in the rest of the saga that follows. Andvari puts a curse on the treasure, saying that whoever owns it will die.

Loki delivers the gold to Hreidmar, who is later killed by his son, Fafnir. Fafnir takes the treasure into the wilderness, where he finds a cave. He puts the treasure into the cave and transforms into a dragon. From then on, Fafnir sleeps in the cave on top of his treasure. Regin says that by taking the treasure, Fafnir has deprived him of his rightful inheritance and forced him to go to the king to ask for employment.

After he has heard the tale, Sigurd becomes angry on Regin's behalf and asks the smith to make him a sword because he has now sworn to kill Fafnir. Regin does so, but when Sigurd smites an anvil with it, the sword shatters. The same thing happens to the second sword. Sigurd then goes to his mother and asks for the shards of the sword Gram, which had belonged to his father. Sigurd brings the shards to Regin and has Gram reforged. When Gram has been made whole, Sigurd tries it against the anvil as he had done with the other swords, and this time the anvil is cloven in two.

Regin reminds Sigurd that he promised to slay Fafnir if Regin made him a sword. Sigurd says that he will keep his promise, but not before he avenges his father, who had been killed in a battle against King Lyngvi. Sigurd goes to Lyngvi's country and begins to pillage and burn. Lyngvi comes against Sigurd with his army, which Sigurd defeats with the help of his friends. At the end of the battle, Sigurd kills Lyngvi.

Sigurd then goes home and tells Regin that he will keep his word about Fafnir. Regin tells Sigurd to dig a pit next to the river and wait for Fafnir to pass over it when he goes to get a drink. When Fafnir's belly is over the pit, Sigurd is to stab him in the heart and so kill him. Sigurd tells Regin that he thinks this a bad plan because the dragon's blood will flow into the pit and drown him. Regin taunts Sigurd, saying that he is a coward and no Volsung.

Stung by this, Sigurd resolves to dig the pit and take his chances. While he is digging, Regin runs away and hides. Then an old man walks up and asks what Sigurd is doing. When Sigurd explains his plan, the old man tells him to dig more than one pit so that the blood will go into the others but not into the one Sigurd sits in.

Sigurd finishes the pits and chooses one to wait in. When the dragon goes to the river, it passes over the pit Sigurd is sitting in. Sigurd thrusts his sword up to the hilt into the dragon's armpit. The dragon writhes away in agony. Sigurd jumps out of the pit and gets his sword back, but when he does this, his arms get covered with the dragon's blood.

As the dragon is dying, it asks Sigurd who he is. At first, Sigurd evades the question and calls himself the "Noble Beast," but eventually he tells Fafnir his name and lineage. As Fafnir is dying, he lays a curse on his treasure.

Once Fafnir is dead, Regin returns. He cuts out Fafnir's heart and drinks some of the dragon's blood. Then he hands the heart to Sigurd and asks him to roast it for him, which Sigurd does. When the heart is nearly roasted, Sigurd touches it to see whether it is cooked and burns his finger. He puts his finger in his mouth, and because it has the dragon's blood on it, Sigurd gains the ability to understand the speech of birds. The birds prophesize about Sigurd's future. They say that Regin intends to betray him and that Sigurd should kill him. Regin takes the birds' advice and cuts off Regin's head. Sigurd eats part of the roasted dragon's heart and keeps the rest for later. Then he goes to Fafnir's lair and takes all the treasure. Among the gold, he finds a helm of terror and other enchanted weaponry. Fafnir's gold is as much as two or three horses could carry, but Grani can carry it all by himself, and Sigurd besides.

Sigurd leaves Fafnir's cave. He discovers the sleeping Brynhild, dressed in armor and lying on a rampart of shields. At first, Sigurd thinks Brynhild is a man, but when he removes her helmet, he discovers she is a woman. Sigurd then removes Brynhild's armor, cutting open her chainmail with his sword. Brynhild wakes up and asks whether the man who cut her armor open is Sigurd. Sigurd says yes.

Brynhild explains that she is a Valkyrie who Odin put into an enchanted sleep because she had killed someone Odin didn't want killed. Odin also made it her fate to marry. Brynhild tells Sigurd that she agreed to Odin's terms, but that she will only marry a man who has no fear, and the only man like that is Sigurd son of Sigmund. Sigurd then asks Brynhild to teach him wise things, and she replies with an extended poem about runes and how they can work different kinds of magic. Sigurd answers with a verse of his own, thanking Brynhild. Brynhild then goes on (in prose) to give Sigurd all kinds of good advice. Sigurd is so impressed he proposes to Brynhild, and she accepts.

Sigurd leaves Brynhild and rides to the court of a king named Heimer, who is married to Brynhild's sister. Sigurd is made very welcome. Some time later, Brynhild arrives at Heimer's court and takes up residence in a separate part of the estate. Sigurd sees her one day and his love for her is rekindled. He goes to visit her and tries to convince her to honor the promise they made to one another and marry him, but Brynhild says that they are not fated to marry one another. Brynhild tells Sigurd that he will marry Gudrun, the daughter of King Gjuki. Sigurd insists that he will marry Brynhild and gives her a gold ring as a pledge of his fidelity; the ring is Andvaranaut, the cursed ring from Fafnir's hoard. Brynhild also pledges her troth.

One day, Gudrun comes to visit Brynhild at Heimer's court. Gudrun and Brynhild talk about famous warriors, and Brynhild praises Sigurd and his prowess. Gudrun tells Brynhild about a dream she had, which Brynhild interprets as foretelling the future, saying that Gudrun will marry Sigurd and that many other woes will befall because of it. Gudrun becomes very sad after hearing this.

Sigurd leaves Heimer's court and goes to Gjuki's, where he is made very welcome, and he becomes friends with Gudrun's brothers, Gunnar and Hogni. Gudrun's mother, Grimhild, wants Sigurd as a husband for her daughter, so she gives Sigurd a drink spiked with a potion that makes him forget Brynhild and then encourages her husband to get Sigurd to marry their daughter. Gjuki agrees, and at a feast after Sigurd drinks the potion, Gjuki offers him Gudrun's hand. Sigurd accepts, and Gunnar and Hogni swear brotherhood to him.

Grimhild then goes to Gunnar and encourages him to seek Brynhild's hand. They go to Brynhild's father, King Budli, and ask whether Gunnar can wed Brynhild. Budli agrees, as long as Brynhild will accept. Sigmund and Gunnar then go to Heimer's estate, where Brynhild is living in a hall that is protected by a wall of flame. When Gunnar cannot ride through the flames, he exchanges shapes with Sigurd. Sigurd rides through the flames in Gunnar's form and woos Brynhild as though he were Gunnar. Brynhild is reluctant to say yes; she is a Valkyrie, after all, and wants to go back to battle. Sigurd, who is wearing Gunnar's body and speaking and acting as though he were Gunnar, reminds her that she said she would marry the man who could ride through the flames, and Brynhild replies that she will keep that promise. Sigurd takes the ring Andvaranaut from Brynhild and gives her another ring from Fafnir's hoard in exchange.

Remaining in Gunnar's form, Sigurd stays with Brynhild for four days, and when they sleep together, he puts a naked sword between them. Sigurd rides back to his friends and changes shapes again with Gunnar. Brynhild goes to Heimer and tells him she is pregnant with a daughter, Aslaug, and makes Heimer Aslaug's foster-father. Brynhild, Gunnar, and Sigurd return to King Budli's court, where Brynhild's marriage to Gunnar is celebrated. During the feast, Sigurd's memory returns, and he realizes what he has done.

Some time after the wedding, Gudrun and Brynhild go down to the river together to swim. Gudrun shows Brynhild the ring Andvaranaut, which Sigurd has given her; Brynhild recognizes the ring but says nothing. Later, Gudrun and Brynhild have an argument over who has the better husband. Gudrun says that she knows about Sigurd's vows to Brynhild and taunts her with the story of Gunnar and Sigurd changing shapes so that Gunnar might marry Brynhild. Brynhild warns Gudrun that she will pay for her malice and the betrayal Brynhild has suffered at the hands of Gudrun and her family, but she also says that she loves Gunnar and intends to be faithful to him.

Brynhild takes to her bed. When Gunnar asks what is wrong, Brynhild says that she knows about Gunnar's deception and how he changed shapes with Sigurd. She says that she is downcast because she has broken her vow to Sigurd and that she did not marry the man she was supposed to have married. When Brynhild threatens to kill both Sigurd and Gunnar, Hogni has her chained up, but Gunnar lets her go.

After that point, Brynhild goes into mourning. Gudrun tries to cheer her up but fails, as does Gunnar. Hogni tries next, with no result. Gunnar asks Sigurd to visit her, but Sigurd gives no reply. The next day, Sigurd does visit her and tries to cheer her up. Brynhild reproaches him for betraying her. They argue, and Brynhild says that she wishes she could kill Sigurd. Sigurd confesses that he still loves Brynhild deeply and wants her to be his wife. Brynhild says that she will not leave Gunnar. Sigurd protests that he was bewitched when he came to Gjuki's court and that none of the deception was his fault. Brynhild says that she wants neither Sigurd nor Gunnar now.

After Sigurd leaves, Gunnar goes to talk to Brynhild. Brynhild prophesies that because of what happened, one of the three of them will die. Either it will be Brynhild herself, or else it will be Gunnar or Sigurd. Later, Brynhild tells Gunnar that she will go back to Heimer's court and stay there forever if Gunnar doesn't kill Sigurd, but Gunnar can't do that because he has sworn an oath of brotherhood with Sigurd. Gunnar confers with Hogni about what to do. They agree to ask their younger brother, Guttorm, to do the deed since he didn't swear the oath. Their justification for killing Sigurd is that he had sex with Brynhild during the four days he was in Brynhild's home.

Gunnar and Hogni prepare enchanted food and drink to make Guttorm turn violent and want to kill Sigurd. Guttorm goes to Sigurd's chamber and stabs Sigurd while he is sleeping with Gudrun next to him. The blow wakens Sigurd, who takes his sword and flings it at Guttorm as Guttorm runs away. The sword cuts Guttorm in half, killing him. Gudrun wakes up and finds herself covered in Sigurd's blood and Sigurd himself dying. As he is dying, Sigurd tells Gudrun that he had only behaved well toward Gunnar and that Brynhild was behind his murder.

Gunnar goes to Brynhild and offers her wergild for Sigurd's death. Brynhild refuses. She then has all her gold brought to her and made into a big pile. She tells everyone that whoever wants some of her gold can take it. Once this is done, she stabs herself in the armpit and prophesies many woes for Gunnar, Gudrun, and all the family of King Gjuki. Then she asks to be burned on a funeral pyre with Sigurd, with a naked sword between them. Gunnar prepares the pyre as she requested, placing upon it Sigurd's body, the body of his young son (who Brynhild also arranged to be murdered), and the body of Guttorm. Once the pyre is lit and roaring flames, Brynhild walks into the fire and lies down beside Sigurd, where she dies.

Part 2: Tales from the Viking Age

Captivating Legendary and Historical Sagas

Introduction

Between the twelfth and the fifteenth centuries, Icelandic scribes were busily at work writing down what had formerly been orally transmitted stories containing both prose and snippets of poetry. Dubbed "sagas"—from the Icelandic *sögur*, meaning "story," "myth," or "history"—the manuscripts diligently copied by medieval scribes preserve histories and pseudo-histories along with imaginative works about dragons, giants, and larger-than-life heroes. Within the total corpus of Icelandic sagas are the *Fornaldursögur*, or "legendary sagas," and the *Íslendingasögur*, or "sagas of Icelanders," which are sometimes also known as "family sagas." These are two of the main subgenres of sagas.

As the name suggests, the legendary sagas are works of fiction. It is in these sagas that we meet all manner of fantastic creatures, read of the exploits of heroes and villains, and occasionally see the gods peek in to steer events or punish evildoers. The sagas of Icelanders, by contrast, are largely historical works that tell the stories of the families who left continental Scandinavian lands to settle Iceland beginning in the late ninth century. However, these historical sagas are not entirely untouched by the fantastic, since they also occasionally contain episodes that involve magic or the supernatural.

Before the advent of Christianity, writing other than runes used for inscriptions or incantations was unknown in Viking lands. Iceland was officially converted to Christianity around the turn of the eleventh century, so the stories that began to be written down in the centuries that followed occasionally are presented through a Christian filter, or have had certain aspects altered in order to conform with Christian doctrine and belief.

This current volume presents three Viking sagas. Two are legendary sagas, while the third is historical. *The Saga of King Heidrek the Wise* centers in part on the dwarf-made magic sword, Tyrfing. Tyrfing was originally made for King Svafrlami, but when he loses it in battle to Arngrim the Berserker, it becomes an heirloom of Arngrim's house, passed down from generation to generation. We can therefore see that even the legendary sagas can conform to certain features of the sagas of Icelanders through a focus on the story of a particular family, following the doings of each successive descendant, who functions as a protagonist in their part of the tale.

The Saga of Örvar-Oddr is a lengthy tale about the exploits of the hero Oddr. Doomed to live a 300-year lifespan only to be killed by a serpent hiding inside the skull of his long-dead horse, Oddr goes from battle to battle and raid to raid, conquering human opponents and giants alike. Oddr lives by both his wits and the strength of his arm which, as we shall see, comes in handy when dealing even with friendly giants. Oddr is something of a peripatetic hero, appearing in other sagas besides his own. We will have already seen Oddr fighting alongside his friend Hjalmar in *The Saga of King Heidrek the Wise* before we encounter him in his own tale.

The final saga in this volume is a historical one, dealing with the late tenth- and early eleventh-century Viking voyages to what is now northeastern Canada. The stories of these voyages are told in two historical works, *The Saga of the Greenlanders* and *The Saga of Eirik the Red*, which together are known as *The Vinland Sagas*. Here, we follow Bjarni Herjolfsson as he discovers this new land when he is blown off course on his way to Greenland, and then the voyages of Eirik's sons and daughter and others of Eirik's Greenland settlement, who make their own attempts to settle in a new place rich in wild grapes, salmon, and other good things.

Whether fantastical or historical, the Viking sagas show us very human characters behaving in very human ways. We see courage and villainy, sorrow and joy, and strength and weakness play out in these complex stories whose creators and first audiences lived over a thousand years ago.

The Saga of King Heidrek the Wise

Like many other Icelandic sagas, The Saga of King Heidrek the Wise—*which is also known as the* Tyrfing Cycle *and the* Heverar Saga—*is not solely about the title character but rather is a tale encompassing the history of several generations of the same family, of which Heidrek is but one descendant. In the first parts of the saga, we learn about Heidrek's forebears and about the history of the enchanted sword, Tyrfing. The earliest sections of the saga are relatively short, but each successive section increases in length until we get to the portion that deals with Heidrek himself, which forms the bulk of the narrative.*

At first, it might seem difficult to understand how Heidrek merits the nickname "the Wise." Heidrek is malicious and impulsive, delighting in starting fights and sowing dissension among the men of his father's court. His final mischievous act at that court is to throw a stone that accidentally kills his brother, which leads to Heidrek's banishment. Before Heidrek is forced to leave, his father gives him some advice, which Heidrek vows to disregard. In the story that follows, we see how Heidrek's disregard for rules turns into a kind of wisdom all its own, although in the end, Heidrek must pay a heavy price for his ruthlessness and overweening pride.

Some readers may see echoes of this saga in the works of J. R. R. Tolkien. The magic sword Tyrfing seems to have been an inspiration for the elven swords that glow in the presence of orcs and that can slice through almost anything with ease, while Heidrek's riddle contest with Gestumblindi (literally "the blind guest") is reminiscent of Bilbo's exchange of riddles with Gollum in The Hobbit.

The version of Heidrek's saga presented here has been abridged to fit this book. Only a small number of the riddles in Heidrek's riddle contest with Gestumblindi have been included, and the part of the saga that tells what happened after Heidrek's death has been omitted except for a brief synopsis. The history of the kings of Sweden that ends the saga has been omitted entirely.

Of Svafrlami

Once there was a king named Svafrlami. He was the son of King Sigrlami, who was the grandson of Odin. Svafrlami liked nothing better than to ride to the hunt with his friends. Often he could be found in the forest, his lance at the ready, and he rarely came home empty-handed.

One day, Svafrlami went out hunting, but as the day wore on, he became separated from his friends, and he found himself in a part of the forest he did not recognize. As the sun was setting, he came upon a large stone that stood in front of a cliff face. Two dwarves were standing outside the stone and clearly were making ready to enter the cleft behind it and so go to their homes. Svafrlami spurred his horse, and when he arrived at the stone, he jumped down quickly and put his sword between the dwarves and the stone.

The dwarves were afraid of this big, strong man who wielded a bright sword and rode a swift horse. "Please, do not kill us!" they begged. "We are just trying to go home! Let us go in peace!"

"First you must tell me your names," said Svafrlami.

"I am Dvalin," said one dwarf, "and this is my brother, Dulin."

"Ah, I have heard tell of you," said Svafrlami. "I have heard that you are the most cunning smiths in the world. I will let you go if you make me a sword the likes of which has never been seen. The blade must be so sharp that it can slice through the strongest steel as though it were parchment, and never will it have any speck of rust. The sword also shall make me invincible; I shall never lose a battle while I wield it, and never shall it miss a blow."

The dwarves reluctantly agreed to make the sword and set a day for the king to return to fetch it. Then the dwarves went into their mountain home, and Svafrlami rode away to find his way back to his own stronghold.

When the day came for the dwarves to give the sword to the king, Svafrlami arrived at the stone in the mountains to find Dvalin and Dulin standing outside, and in Dvalin's hands was the most beautiful sword Svafrlami had ever seen. It had a sheath and belt of the finest leather, and its golden hilt gleamed in the sun.

Dvalin gave the sword to the king and said, "Here is the sword you demanded. I give it to you as agreed, but to you I also say this: every time the sword is drawn, it must taste blood, and it must be sheathed again with that blood still upon it. Three crimes will be committed with this sword, and in the end, the sword will be the death of you yourself."

Svafrlami drew the sword and swung it at the dwarves, but they were too quick. Before the blow could land upon them, Dvalin and Dulin slipped into their mountain home, and the sword buried itself deep in the heavy stone that was their door. Svafrlami pulled the sword out of the stone, sheathed it, then mounted his horse and rode away, pleased with the dwarves' craftsmanship and scoffing at the curse they had laid upon him and upon the sword. The king named the sword Tyrfing, and whenever he carried it into battle, he was the victor.

Svafrlami married and became the father of a beautiful daughter named Eyfura. For a long time, Svafrlami's lands were peaceful and safe, for every time a foe assailed them, Svafrlami would challenge the other king to single combat. With the aid of the sword Tyrfing, Svafrlami conquered every enemy that dared take up his challenge.

This went on for many, many years, until Svafrlami was an old man. One day, a Viking named Arngrim left his stronghold on the island of Bolm and sailed to Svafrlami's lands, thinking to raid and pillage wherever he wished. When Svafrlami heard of Arngrim's arrival, he sent out a challenge to single combat, as was his wont. Arngrim accepted the challenge and met Svafrlami on the field of battle at the appointed time. The two warriors circled one another, holding up their shields and feinting with their swords while their armies stood at either side of the field, looking on. Soon the battle was joined in earnest, but it wasn't long until Svafrlami made one great sweep with his blade that sliced off the side of Arngrim's shield. Unfortunately for Svafrlami, the blow was aimed with such strength that the sword continued downward until its point became lodged in the earth. Arngrim seized upon this advantage by cutting off Svafrlami's hand at the wrist and taking Tyrfing for himself. Then Arngrim took Tyrfing and clove Svafrlami's body in two with it, and in this way part of the dwarves' curse came to pass, that Svafrlami himself would be killed by that enchanted blade.

With Svafrlami defeated, Arngrim and his warriors attacked Svafrlami's men, and soon Arngrim's army had the victory and went through the lands pillaging and taking captives, and there was none to stand against them. One of the captives was Svafrlami's daughter, Eyfura. Arngrim took her for his wife, and together they returned to his stronghold on Bolm.

Of the Sons of Arngrim

Arngrim and Eyfura together had twelve sons. The eldest was named Angantyr, and after him followed in turn Hervarth, Hjörvarth, Saeming, Hrani, Brami, Barri, Reifnir, Tind, and Bui. There were also the twins, both named Hadding, who were the youngest children of the family. When all the boys had grown into men, Angantyr was the tallest and the strongest of all of them, while the twins were the smallest and the weakest.

But even the weakest of Arngrim's sons was stronger than most other men, and together the twelve brothers often took ship to go raiding in other lands. Never did they take anyone else with them, for no other help was needed, and they always came home with their ship heavily laden with booty. Soon they were so greatly feared that whenever their sail appeared on the horizon, the king of that place and his people would crowd onto the beach and there make a pile of their greatest treasures, so that the sons of Arngrim might take the gold and jewels and other goods and then leave without killing or taking captives or setting fire to roof and rick.

Now, each of Arngrim's sons had his own sword, and some of these swords became famous in story and song. Angantyr received Tyrfing as an heirloom from his father. Hervarth's sword was named Hrotti, and Saeming's was called Mistiltein. Tyrfing was the most powerful of all. It gleamed with a silver light when it was unsheathed, a light that came from the blade itself and that could even illuminate the darkness. Never could the wielder of Tyrfing return the sword to its sheath unless it had fresh blood upon the blade, and whoever the sword struck perished of the wound before the end of the next day, even if the wound was but very slight.

One Yule, the sons of Arngrim sat feasting and drinking, as was their custom. At the end of the feast, they passed around the pledge cup so that vows for the coming year might be made. When Hjörvarth received the cup, he said, "I vow that I shall go to Sweden and wed the daughter of King Yngvi. Ingeborg is the most beautiful maiden in the whole world, and only she is worthy to be my wife." Then Hjörvarth drank of the pledge cup, and so his vow was sealed.

The following spring, Hjörvarth and his brothers took ship for Uppsala. They went to King Yngvi's court, where they were well received. Yngvi granted them an audience in the chamber where he sat with his wisest advisers and bravest warriors, and at the king's side sat the lovely Ingeborg.

"Tell me who you are and what your errand is," said Yngvi, "and I will decide what is to be done about it."

Hjörvarth stood forth and said, "I am Hjörvarth, son of Arngrim. I have come to ask for the hand of your daughter, Ingeborg, in marriage."

"I see," said Yngvi, but before the king could say anything else, Hjalmar, Yngvi's bravest warrior, stood and said, "I ask you to let me speak, O King." The king nodded assent, so Hjalmar continued: "I have served you for a long time. I have fought to protect your people and your lands. I have taken wounds and shed blood on your behalf. I ask that you grant Ingeborg's hand to me, and not to this stranger whose life is spent in murder and theft."

Now Yngvi found himself in a quandary. If he gave his daughter to Hjörvarth, he would lose Hjalmar's loyalty and blood would be shed. If he gave his daughter to Hjalmar, Hjörvarth and his brothers would not leave until every last person in that chamber had been hacked to pieces and the stronghold looted and burned. Finally the king said, "You are both worthy suitors, but it is not my choice to make. Ingeborg must be the one to decide."

Ingeborg said, "If it is to be my choice, then I choose Hjalmar. I know him to be a good and honorable man. I would have a husband who knows what honor is, not some berserker whose hands are stained with the blood of so many."

Hjörvarth replied, "Very well, if that is your wish then so shall it be. But I challenge Hjalmar to meet me in single combat at midsummer. We will meet in Samsø. If you do not come, Hjalmar, I shall make sure that every man, woman, and child throughout every land knows that you are a rank coward and unfit to be wed to a highborn lady such as Ingeborg. You will not be able to show your face anywhere at all for shame."

"I am no coward," said Hjalmar. "I will meet you in Samsø at midsummer, and we shall see then who prevails."

Hjörvarth and his brothers sailed home and told their father all that had happened in Uppsala. "I like it not," said Arngrim when he had heard the tale. "Never yet have I had any cause to fear for any of my sons, but this to me bodes ill. Still, there is nothing to be done now; you must follow through with your challenge, Hjörvarth, or be named a coward yourself."

The sons of Arngrim stayed at their father's house throughout the winter. In the spring, they took ship for Samsø. On the way, they stopped at the stronghold of Earl Bjartmar, who had long been friends with Arngrim and his sons. Bjartmar caused a great feast to be held in honor of the twelve young men, and at the feast Angantyr asked for the hand of the earl's daughter, Svafa, in marriage. The earl and his daughter both consented, and so she and Angantyr were wed with great rejoicing.

Soon it was time for the sons of Arngrim to go to Samsø. Before boarding the ship, Angantyr asked to speak to his father-in-law. "My lord," said Angantyr, "I had a strange dream last night. I hear you are wise in these matters, so perhaps you might be able to tell me what it means."

"Tell me your dream, and I will do what I can," said the earl.

"I dreamed that we were on Samsø. There were a great many birds there, and my brothers and I slew them all. As we prepared to leave, two great eagles swooped down upon us. I fought with one eagle, and my brothers all fought against the other. But we were weak from having killed all the other birds, and so we all were overcome."

"There is no secret to this dream," said the earl. "It foretells the death of twelve fierce warriors."

Angantyr and his brothers then sailed for Samsø. When they arrived, they saw two ships in the harbor and rightly guessed that these were Hjalmar's ships. In fact, only one was Hjalmar's; the other belonged to Hjalmar's friend, Örvar-Oddr, who had come to Samsø to lend his support to Hjalmar if it was needed.

When the sons of Arngrim saw those ships, the berserker rage came over them. They boarded the ships, and although Hjalmar and Oddr's men fought bravely, they could not withstand Angantyr and his brothers. Soon every man aboard the ships had been slain, and the sons of Arngrim were roaring their way inland in search of Hjalmar.

Now, Hjalmar and Oddr had not been on the ships when the brothers arrived. They had gone ashore and walked inland, thinking to await Hjörvarth and thus be ready for the combat. Time passed, and when the challenger and his brothers had not arrived, Hjalmar and Oddr decided to walk back down to the shore to see whether anything had happened there. Not far from the beach, they came across the sons of Arngrim. The berserker rage had left them, making them weaker than they were at other times, and their swords were drenched in blood, telling the tale of their deeds upon the ships.

Hjalmar and Oddr paused. "Do you see what has befallen?" said Hjalmar. "They have already slain all our men and are likely to slay us as well. Doubtless we will be drinking ale with Odin in Valhalla tonight."

Oddr replied, "Valhalla may be a glorious place and Odin a gracious host, but I have other plans for tonight. We will kill each and every one of those berserkers, even though there are only two of us and twelve of them."

Heartened by Oddr's words, Hjalmar said, "So be it. We fight with those twelve, and we see who shall have the victory." Then Hjalmar said, "Look! Angantyr carries the sword Tyrfing. See how it shines? How shall we divide the fight? Will you take Angantyr alone and I the other eleven, or should I fight Angantyr and you his brothers?'

"I want to fight Angantyr," said Oddr. "Tyrfing is a mighty blade, to be sure, but my mail shirt is better than yours."

"Maybe so," said Hjalmar, "but I'm the leader here, and it's my honor that is at stake, not yours. I fight Angantyr, and you fight his brothers. I'll not have it said that I was afraid to face Tyrfing."

And so Hjalmar and Oddr went down to the beach and challenged Angantyr and his brothers. Hjalmar fought valiantly against Angantyr, and Oddr fought the other eleven, cutting them down one by one. When the battle was done, Angantyr and all the sons of Arngrim lay dead.

Oddr turned to Hjalmar, who was seated on the grass. "See?" said Oddr. "I knew we would be victorious! But why are you so pale? And your mail shirt is in tatters!"

Hjalmar replied, "I have taken sixteen wounds in my battle with Angantyr. You may not be Odin's guest tonight, but I surely will be. One of those wounds is just beneath my heart." Then Hjalmar took the ring from his finger and gave it to Oddr, saying, "Take this ring back to Ingeborg. Give it to her as a token of my love." Hjalmar took one last breath and then died.

Oddr made barrows for each of Arngrim's sons and laid them therein with all their weapons. Tyrfing was laid in the barrow with Angantyr. When this was done, Oddr took Hjalmar's body back to Sweden to be buried there, but once Ingeborg saw that Hjalmar was dead, she died of a broken heart, and the two were buried together in one grave.

Of Hervor, Who Also Bore the Name Hervarth

In the court of Earl Bjartmar, Angantyr's wife Svafa was with child. When her time came, she gave birth to a baby girl, who she named Hervor. Svafa made her own father Hervor's foster-father, and both of them swore never to tell Hervor about Angantyr, lest she try to avenge him.

Hervor grew up tall and strong, and she had her father's berserker spirit. She was not content to stay at home and learn embroidery and other womanly arts; instead, she took up the bow and the sword and quickly became a more accomplished warrior and hunter than many of the fully grown men at the earl's court. When anyone tried to take away her weapons and set her to her needle, she ran away into the forest, where she lived like a highwayman, robbing any who came within sight. When the earl found out what Hervor had been doing, he sent men to the forest to capture her and bring her back to his court by force.

For a time, Hervor dwelt in her grandfather's house, but she was no more peaceful there than she had been in the forest. Often she amused herself by tormenting the slaves of the household. For a time, the slaves bore this ill-treatment without saying anything, but finally one of them could hold her peace no longer. "You are an evil person, Hervor, and you spend all your days doing evil things. But I suppose this is to be expected, given your parentage. Do you know why your grandfather has never mentioned your father's name? It's because he was nothing but a lowly swineherd, and you, in turn, have inherited that low nature."

Hervor then ran to her grandfather and demanded to be told the truth. "Was my father truly a swineherd? Am I truly the daughter of such a low-born churl?"

Bjartmar sighed. "No, Hervor, you are not the daughter of a swineherd. You are the daughter of Angantyr, son of Arngrim, and the blood of berserkers flows in your veins. Your father and his brothers were slain in battle on the island of Samsø before you were born."

When Hervor heard this, she dressed herself in men's clothing and found herself a sword and a bow with a quiver of arrows. She went to her mother and grandfather and said, "I can remain here no longer. I will take ship and live the life of a Viking. I will seek out the barrows of my father and my uncles. I will take Tyrfing for my own, and then I will avenge my father and all his brothers."

Hervor's mother and grandfather tried to change her mind, but Hervor would not be swayed. She changed her name to Hervarth and went down to the harbor, where she found a ship and a crew who were willing to go raiding with her. They sailed from place to place, looting as they went, but always Hervarth was thinking of her father and her uncles and what she must do to avenge them.

One night, Hervarth went to the captain of the ship and said, "We must sail to Samsø."

"I'll not sail there," said the captain. "That place has an ill name. It is haunted with all manner of spirits. If we go there, none of us will leave alive."

"We sail where I say we sail," said Hervarth. "And if you and the others are too cowardly to go ashore, you can wait for me in the ship. What I must do I must do alone, in any case."

"Very well," said the captain, "but if it goes ill for you with the spirits, we'll not come to fetch your body. You can rot there and be food for the ravens, if the spirits don't devour you first."

And so they sailed for Samsø, but when they arrived, the captain would not sail to the dock but rather anchored the ship in the harbor just as the sun was beginning to set. Hervarth took one of the small rowboats they had aboard and went ashore by herself. She began to walk inland, and soon came upon a shepherd gathering up his flock for the night.

"You there!" said Hervarth. "Can you tell me where the barrows of Hjörvarth and his brothers might be?"

"I can tell you," said the shepherd, "but if you have any sense, you'll stay far away from that place. And don't you see the sun is setting? It's not safe to be out after nightfall here. You should go back to wherever you came from."

"That I'll not," said Hervarth. "I fear neither man nor spirit. Now tell me, where are the barrows?"

"They are over there, beyond the forest," said the shepherd. "You'll know them by the flame that burns around them, night and day. Now, if you don't have the sense to go inside before it gets dark, I do."

Without another word, the shepherd called to his dogs and his sheep and set off for home.

Hervarth walked in the direction the shepherd had shown her, and soon enough she saw the light of the flames around the barrows. When Hervarth drew near, she saw that the fire was not something made and tended by human hands. Although the flames leapt high into the air, they did not consume anything around them, not even the dry grass at their feet.

Hervarth went through the wall of flames without fear and stood before the barrows of the twelve brothers. She looked upon the barrows for a moment, and then said:

Wake, Angantyr!
Sfava's daughter
says to you, "Wake!"
Your only child, Hervor,
is here to wake you.
Wake, Angantyr!
Wake Saeming!
Wake Hjörvarth!
Give me the sword
with the bright edge
and the golden hilt,
the sword forged by Dvalin
for Svafrlami.

When Hervarth was done with her incantation, the earth of one of the barrows stirred. A mist gathered on top of it, and from the mist arose the shade of Angantyr. The shade looked at Hervarth and said:

Why wake me?

Why are you here?

Daughter mine,

this is no place for the living.

The blade you seek

is not here.

No kinsman buried me;

an enemy placed me here.

He placed me in my barrow,

the sword he bore away with him.

Seek it not!

It will be your doom.

Then Hervarth said:

I fear no doom,

nor the words of a shade.

Tell me no lies!

Give me the sword!

It is my birthright,

and it lies there

with you in your barrow.

Angantyr replied:

The sword shall you have

but not before

I speak to you your doom.

A son you shall have,
Heidrek will he be named.
Tyrfing will be his blade,
the strongest of men shall he be.
The blade is here,
beneath my back,
enwrapped in flame.
No woman has courage
enough to take it.
Hervarth answered,
Courage I have,
enough to take the sword.
I can see it now,
sheathed in flames.
If you will not yield it,
I will take it myself.
Even now
the flames subside
as I reach toward your barrow.
Then the shade of Angantyr said,
Very well!
Take it not;
I will give it you.
But it will bring only sorrow,
only grief, only ruin
to you and to yours.
Fare you well!

Would that I and my brothers
could rise and walk with you.
But that is not our fate.
Fare you well!

When the shade of Angantyr finished speaking, it dissolved into mist. The mist dissolved back into the earth, and in its place atop the barrow was Tyrfing, with its sheath and belt. Hervarth took the sword and said:

Fare you well!
May you rest here
undisturbed.
Go I must;
the barrow is no place
for a living woman.
Fare you well!

Then Hervarth walked back through the wall of flames and set off through the forest. It had been a long journey to the barrows, and it was a long journey back. By the time she reached the shore, the sun was already peeking above the horizon, and in the dawn's light, Hervarth saw that her ship had already left the harbor, stranding her there on the island. She then went to the nearest village, where she was able to buy passage back to the mainland.

Hervarth traveled until she came to the court of King Gudmund. There she tarried for a time, but since she was still clad in men's raiment and still calling herself by a man's name, no one recognized that she was a woman. Gudmund and his courtiers were gracious to Hervarth, and treated her as though she were a man like themselves.

One day, Gudmund was playing chess and found that he was likely to lose. He sighed and then said, "I seem to be overmatched. Can no one here rescue me and turn the game to my favor?"

"I can do that, my lord," said Hervarth, and so Gudmund gave her his seat and she began to play. It did not take long for Hervarth to reverse the king's fortunes, but as she played, one of the courtiers took up her sword from the place she had laid it and turned it over in his hands, admiring the craftsmanship of the sheath and the hilt. Then the courtier drew the sword and said, "Here is a most noble blade, indeed! I have never seen one so fine!"

Now, Hervarth had been so engrossed in the game that she did not notice the courtier had Tyrfing in his hands until he drew it and began exclaiming. Straight away, Hervarth went to the courtier, wrested the sword from his grasp, and then struck off his head with the blade. She picked up the scabbard and belt, sheathed the sword, and left Gudmund's court.

All of Gudmund's warriors clamored to be allowed to follow Hervarth to have vengeance for killing their companion, but Gudmund would not allow it. "There is more to that Hervarth than meets the eye," he said, "and you will have small fame for his death, not least because I suspect that he is a woman. That woman is in possession of a mighty sword, and doubtless knows how to use it; I fear none of you would return alive from that quest. So this is my final word: no one will follow Hervarth. She leaves my court in peace."

For a time, Hervarth went raiding with the Vikings, but soon she became weary of that life. She took ship to her grandfather's court, where she was joyfully received by the earl and by her mother. Hervarth set aside her men's raiment and put on women's garb. She took her own name back and began to work at her embroidery. Soon the tale of the beautiful woman who had arrived at the earl's court made its way throughout the lands, and many young men thought to ask for her hand in marriage.

Now, King Gudmund had a son named Höfund, and he was a man both strong and wise. One day, Höfund went to his father and said, "Father, it is time that I took a wife. I come to you to ask your aid in this. Who would it be best for me to marry?"

King Gudmund said, "I know none who is more worthy than Hervor, granddaughter of Earl Bjartmar. It is she who should become your wife."

Höfund agreed to this, and soon King Gudmund sent emissaries to Bjartmar's court on that errand. Bjartmar received them well, and when Hervor learned that Höfund asked for her hand, she agreed to marry him. Soon all was prepared, and Höfund and Hervor were wed with great joy and feasting, and they lived together happily as man and wife.

Of Heidrek

Höfund was the wisest of men, and all the people praised his good judgment. He was so wise that judges ever after were known as "höfund" in his honor. Whenever Höfund made a ruling, none dared go against it.

Höfund and Hervor had two sons. The elder was named Angantyr, and the younger was named Heidrek. Both of them grew into strong men, tall and fair of face. Angantyr took after his father. He was wise and wanted to do right by everyone. But Heidrek, whose foster-father was the hero Gizur, was the opposite. Heidrek was cunning and crafty, and he happily sowed dissension wherever he could.

There came a time when Höfund had a feast in his stronghold. He invited everyone to come and partake of the feast, except for Heidrek. When Heidrek found out about this, he was very angry and decided to go to the feast whether he had been invited or not. He also wanted to make mischief among his father's men in revenge for the slight.

Heidrek went to Höfund's stronghold and strode into the great hall as though he belonged there. Höfund and the other men glowered at Heidrek, not simply because he dared appear uninvited, but also because they knew no good would come of his presence there. Angantyr, however, rose and greeted his brother and gave him a seat beside him at the table. Heidrek took no joy in this, but rather sat there scowling.

After a time, Angantyr left the feast. Heidrek began to talk to the men who were seated on either side of him, lacing his talk with ill words that made one man think that the other was insulting him, while keeping himself out of the dispute. Soon the argument rose to such a pitch that it came to blows. Heidrek kept clear of the fighting, sitting back with silent pleasure at the malice he had wrought.

While the fight was still going on, Angantyr came back into the hall.

"What is this?" he said. "Why do you fight here in my father's hall, where all should be at peace with one another?"

The men stopped fighting and went back to their seats, but they were not at peace with one another.

After a little while, Angantyr left again, and Heidrek reminded the men about their argument. This caused the fight to resume, and it did not cease until Angantyr returned and told them both to make peace with one another. Again, Angantyr went out, and again Heidrek goaded the men into an argument. This time, one of the men took his knife and slew the other. Angantyr was very angry at what had happened, and when Höfund learned of it, he told Heidrek to go home and to stop making trouble.

Heidrek went out of the hall and Angantyr went with him, and they said their farewells to one another in the forecourt. Heidrek walked away, but he hadn't gone far when he decided there was yet more mischief to be made. He looked about on the ground and found a large stone. He listened and could hear people speaking to one another outside the hall. Heidrek hefted the stone in his hand, then threw it in the direction of the voices. From the sounds that followed, Heidrek knew that the stone had hit someone. He went to see who had been struck, and when he found that he had killed his brother, he ran away into the forest.

Heidrek regretted his deed, so in the morning he went back into the hall and told the whole tale to his father and mother. When Höfund heard the story, he became very angry indeed. "This is a foul deed you have done, Heidrek, fouler than any other mischief you have accomplished so far. You have not only struck down a man from afar without giving him the chance to defend himself, but you have struck down your only brother. You deserve to hang for this, but I will not pass that sentence. Rather, you shall be an outlaw. Leave my realm, and never return, on pain of death."

Hervor was troubled by Höfund's judgment, for of her two sons she loved Heidrek best. "Surely, husband, this sentence is much too harsh? Should our son not be permitted to return to his parents at some time? Is he to lose all his inheritance?"

"My judgment stands, wife," said Höfund. "Heidrek is an outlaw from this point forth."

"If you will not relent," said Hervor, "then at least give him some good advice before he departs."

"He does not deserve anything, not even good words," said Höfund, "but because you ask, I will give."

Höfund turned to Heidrek and said, "Here is my advice, although I doubt very much that you will follow it. First, never help a man who has betrayed his lord. Second, never protect a murderer. Third, do not let your wife go home to visit her relatives, no matter how she might beg for this. Fourth, do not dally overlate with your mistress. Fifth, when you are in a hurry, do not ride your best horse. Sixth, do not be a foster-father to the child of a man who is of a higher status than yourself. That is all my advice, though likely you reckon it of little value."

Heidrek said, "I hold your advice in low regard because it was given with ill will. I am not obliged to follow even one word of it."

Then Heidrek turned on his heel and left the hall, and in a moment his mother followed him.

"Heidrek, my son," said Hervor, "you have truly done yourself ill this time. Höfund will never relent, and you will never be able to return. But I will give you some gifts before you depart. Here is a purse full of gold, and here is a sword. This sword is Tyrfing, and it once belonged to my father, Angantyr the berserker. It is a famous blade; everyone has heard of it. It is also a victorious blade; whenever you draw it, you will be victorious. Now you must go. Farewell." Then Hervor went back into the hall, and Heidrek walked away to find his fortune as an outlaw.

After Heidrek had been journeying for some time, he came across a group of men. One of the men was bound with ropes.

"What has this man done that you bind him so?" asked Heidrek.

"He betrayed his lord," said one of the men of the group.

"Will you accept ransom for him?" said Heidrek. "I'll give you half of the gold in my purse if you let him go."

The men conferred among themselves and then said they agreed to Heidrek's terms. Heidrek gave them the gold, and then they lost the other from his bonds.

"Thank you for sparing me," said the man who had been bound. "In return for your kindness, I offer you my service."

"That service I'll not accept," said Heidrek. "A man who is willing to betray his own lord is likely to do the same to me. Go your own way; I never want to see you again."

Heidrek resumed his journey, and soon he came upon another group of men leading another man who was bound with ropes, as the first had been.

"What has this man done that you bind him so?" asked Heidrek.

"He is a murderer," said one of the men of the group.

"Will you accept ransom for him?" said Heidrek. "I'll give you half of the gold in my purse if you let him go."

The men conferred among themselves and then said they agreed to Heidrek's terms. Heidrek gave them the gold, and then they lost the other from his bonds.

"Thank you for sparing me," said the man who had been bound. "In return for your kindness, I offer you my service."

"That service I'll not accept," said Heidrek. "Someone who is willing to murder one man is likely to do the same to me. Go your own way; I never want to see you again."

Heidrek wandered the world for a long time until he finally came to Reidgotaland, where a man named Harald was king, who made Heidrek very welcome. Harald was now of a great age, and he sorrowed that he had no heir to take the throne after him. But that was not the end of Harald's troubles. Some of his earls had risen up against him, and in order to prevent war and the loss of his throne, Harald had agreed to pay them heavy tribute.

One day, Heidrek saw a great pile of treasure being heaped up in the forecourt of Harald's stronghold. Heidrek went to Harald and said, "What is this? Is this tribute that you are receiving from lands you have conquered?"

"Would that it were so!" said Harald. "But alas, no. This is tribute I must pay to my earls."

"Surely this is a shameful thing for a king such as yourself!" said Heidrek. "Why do you not resist?"

"Because this is the price of peace. I am too old to fight them any longer, and I do not wish them to wreak havoc among my people if I fail to pay. Besides, when I have faced them in the past, it has gone ill with me and my men."

"My lord, let me lead your army against these earls," said Heidrek. "I owe you a debt of gratitude for your hospitality, and it pains me to see a king of so great a kingdom reduced to paying tribute to his own earls."

"Very well," said the king. "You may lead my army against them, and if you defeat these earls, your reward will be great indeed. But I rather fear that it will go ill with you, and that you will not return to my house when all has been done."

Harald then placed his army under Heidrek's command, and all was made ready to assail the lands of the rebellious earls. Heidrek led the army into the territory of one earl after another, pillaging and slaying as they went. When the earls heard what Heidrek's army was doing, they summoned their own host and went out to meet him. Soon the two armies met, and battle was joined. Heidrek rode at the head of his army wielding Tyrfing. Every man that Heidrek faced he slew, for Tyrfing went through helm and shield and mail like a scythe through hay. Heidrek fought his way through the press of men until he found the earls, and then slew every last one of them. When the earls' men saw that their leaders had been killed and that the better part of their army already lay dead on the field, they fled, and the day was Heidrek's.

When the battle was done, Heidrek went throughout the earls' domains and told the people that they now owed tribute to Harald. He collected the tribute and returned in triumph to Harald's stronghold.

"Welcome, indeed!" said Harald when he saw Heidrek's return and the huge amount of treasure he brought with him. "You have saved my kingdom and enriched it besides. Anything you ask for, I will give you."

"I ask the hand of your daughter, Helga, in marriage," said Heidrek, "and for half your kingdom."

"They are both yours, with my blessing and with my great thanks," said the king.

Of Heidrek's Kingship

Heidrek and Helga lived together very happily. They had one son, whom they named Angantyr, and Harald in his old age finally had a son of his own, who was named Halfdan.

For a time, all went well in Reidgotaland. Heidrek and Harald ruled wisely and well, and the people prospered. But then a great famine came, a famine such as no one could remember having come before. King Harald and Heidrek went to the soothsayers to ask what might be done because their people were starving, and nothing they had tried did any good.

The soothsayers cast lots and read the augury. They told the kings that the only way to appease the gods was to sacrifice the most noble boy in the land.

"Surely your son is the most noble," said Harald. "He should be the one sacrificed."

"No, it is your son who is nobler than mine," said Heidrek. "Halfdan should be the sacrifice."

The two kings argued about this for a long time. Finally, they decided to submit their quarrel to King Höfund, since he was the only one wise enough to judge the case. Heidrek was made leader of the embassy, which included the chiefest nobles and wisest counselors of both his realm and of Harald's. When the embassy arrived at his father's court, they were made very welcome.

Höfund heard the case and then pronounced judgment. He said, "Heidrek's son, Angantyr, is the noblest in the land. It is he who should be sacrificed."

"Very well," said Heidrek, "but if my son is the one to die, what should I get as recompense?"

"You should demand that every other man of the embassy who accompanied you here should be given over to your service," said Höfund. "After that, it will be up to you to decide what is to be done next."

Heidrek and the others went back to Reidgotaland. Heidrek told Harald what the judgment had been, and Harald agreed. He handed over the men to Heidrek, and a time and place were fixed for the sacrifice. But instead of preparing for the ceremony, Heidrek mustered his army and marched on Harald. There was a great battle, and at the end, Heidrek fought and killed Harald. Then Heidrek claimed that all of Harald's realm was now his, and that the sacrifice to Odin was to be the dead who now lay slain on the field. When Helga learned what her husband had done, she was so distraught over the death of her father that she hanged herself.

There came a time when Heidrek summoned his army and went campaigning with them in the south. They went to the land of the Huns, where the king was named Humli. Heidrek defeated Humli and took Humli's daughter, Sifka, captive. For a time, Sifka lived with Heidrek as his mistress, but when she was got with child, Heidrek sent her back to her father. Sifka gave birth to a boy who was given the name Hlöd. Hlöd was raised by his grandfather, Humli, and was said to be the most beautiful child ever to be born.

Another time, Heidrek mustered his army and went to Saxland, thinking to conquer it. When the king of Saxland saw Heidrek's army, he sent an embassy to sue for peace. Heidrek accepted, on condition that the king give his lands to Heidrek and his daughter in marriage besides, for she was a very fair maiden, and Heidrek had heard tell of her great beauty. The king of Saxland agreed, and so there was a great feast held to celebrate the peace and the wedding of Heidrek and the king of Saxland's daughter. Heidrek greatly increased his wealth and his realm on this errand, and had become a very great king thereby.

From time to time, Heidrek's wife would ask leave to go to Saxland to visit her father. Heidrek of course granted her permission since he had yet to go against that piece of Höfund's advice. On these occasions, the queen would often take little Angantyr with her.

One summer, Heidrek had gone out raiding with some of his men. Their journey brought them close to Saxland, so Heidrek decided to row ashore in a little boat, accompanied by one other. They went at night, silently beaching their boat and then creeping toward the king's stronghold. Heidrek and his companion went to the window of the chamber where Heidrek's wife was wont to sleep, and they peered inside. There they saw the queen, asleep in the arms of another man who had long, golden hair. Little Angantyr was in a cot of his own in another part of the room.

"Surely you will slay them both?" said Heidrek's companion. "No king should have to live with that shame."

"No, I'll not slay them," said Heidrek.

"You've killed other men for far less."

"Yes, but I wish to do something else this time."

Heidrek evaded the watchmen and crept silently into the bedchamber. He took his knife and cut a great lock of hair from the man's head without waking either him or the queen. Then Heidrek picked up the sleeping Angantyr and bore him away back to his ships.

In the morning, Heidrek sailed into the harbor and was greeted with great rejoicing. The king of Saxland called for a feast, and when Heidrek was seated in the hall, he said, "I see my lady queen, but where is my son?"

A silence fell.

The queen said, "I have sad news to impart. Angantyr died in the night. That is why he is not here."

"Dead? My son? I don't believe it," said Heidrek. "Show me his body."

The queen brought Heidrek to the place where she said Angantyr's body was. Heidrek undid the wrappings around the corpse and saw that the creature inside was a dog.

"Well!" said Heidrek. "My son truly is in a sorry state, if he is not only dead but also turned into a dog!"

Then Heidrek sent for Angantyr, and when the boy entered the hall, Heidrek produced the lock of hair from his purse and said, "Here you see my son, quite alive, and not a dog at all. Now I would like to know from which of you I took this lock of hair."

Heidrek had the lock of hair matched to every man at the court, but it belonged to none of them. Then Heidrek began looking among the servants and slaves of the place until he came to the kitchen, where one of the slaves had a cloth wrapped around his head. Heidrek tore the cloth off the man's head and held up the lock of hair.

"Surely none will say that this is not his hair," said Heidrek, and everyone had to admit that it did belong to the man.

Heidrek went to the king of Saxland and said, "You have always been a gracious host and have always been at peace with my realm. I'll not make war on you because of this, even though I have just cause. But your daughter I return to you; I want her no longer."

Then Heidrek left that court with Angantyr and sailed back to his own kingdom.

The next summer, Heidrek decided it was time for him to go against another of his father's counsels. Heidrek summoned messengers and sent them to the king of the Gardar in Gardariki to ask to be allowed to foster the king's son. The king of the Gardar heard Heidrek's request and said to the messengers, "I have no mind to send my son to King Heidrek. He is an evil man, cunning and crafty, and I do not wish my son to live with him."

But the queen said, "Think what you are saying, my lord! King Heidrek may have an evil reputation, but he is also a very mighty king, and everyone knows how ruthless he is. If you refuse this request, he may become angry. It will go ill for us then."

And so the king of the Gardar relented and sent his son to be fostered by Heidrek. The young boy was made very welcome in Heidrek's court. Heidrek was a good foster-father to the boy, teaching him all the things he needed to know and loving him as though the boy were his own.

At that time, Sifka, the daughter of Humli, the king of the Huns, had returned to live with Heidrek. Heidrek's counselors did not trust Sifka, and so they told the king not to let her know anything that would better be kept secret. Heidrek said that he understood their concerns and would keep their counsel in mind.

The son of the king of the Gardar had been at Heidrek's court for a few years when a messenger came to invite Heidrek to a feast in Gardariki. Heidrek of course accepted with many thanks. He went to Gardariki, bringing with him the king's son and Sifka. When they arrived, the king of the Gardar made them very welcome, and a great feast was held.

The feast went on for many days, and on one of those days, the men of the court took their hounds and hawks and went out hunting. During the hunt, the men separated into different parties. Some went this way, others went that, and Heidrek and his foster-son soon found themselves alone near a solitary farmstead. Heidrek said to his foster-son, "I have a task for you. Go to that farmstead, and hide yourself well. Stay there until I send for you." Heidrek then removed a ring from his finger and gave it to the boy. "Take this ring as payment. Now go."

The boy hesitated. "I do not think this is proper for me to do," he said, "but since you ask it, I will go."

Heidrek watched until he saw the boy slip into the barn unobserved. Then he returned to the king's court, where he assumed a sorrowful expression and refused company.

Sifka saw Heidrek's demeanor and wondered what was wrong. "Has something happened, my lord?" she said. "Why so sad when all others here are rejoicing?"

"I must not tell you," said Heidrek, "for if word got out, surely the king would have my head struck from my body."

"Come, now," said Sifka, "tell me what is wrong. You know I love you and that I would never betray you."

Heidrek continued to refuse her request while Sifka caressed and kissed him, thinking to persuade him to confess his secret in that way. Finally, Heidrek gave in and said, "I will tell you, but you must not say a word to anyone else. Do you so swear?"

"I so swear," said Sifka. "Now tell me what troubles you."

"My foster-son and I went hunting with the king's men. We found ourselves alone in an apple orchard. The day had been long, and the boy was hungry. He asked me to get him an apple from one of the trees, since he was not tall enough to reach one himself. Without thinking, I drew my sword and cut down an apple for him, but when I went to sheathe the sword, I found I could not do it. Then I remembered Tyrfing's enchantment, that it cannot be sheathed once drawn unless it has tasted blood. So, I cut off the boy's head with the sword and hid the body. That is why I am uneasy, because once the king finds out, he surely will have me killed."

The next day, the king of the Gardar held a drinking party in the great hall. Everyone sat along the tables and drank as much ale as they liked. Sifka was seated next to the queen of the Gardar. The queen turned to Sifka and said, "Your Heidrek certainly is gloomy these days. He's hardly touched his ale at all. What is the matter? Is he ill?"

"Oh, no, my lady," said Sifka, "he is not ill at all. He is sad because he slew your son and is afraid of what will become of him."

Sifka told the queen all that she had learned from Heidrek, and when her tale was done, the queen got up from the table and rushed from the hall, shedding many sorrowful tears. The king saw his queen leave, so he went to Sifka and said, "I saw you holding converse with my lady queen. What did you say to her to distress her so?"

"If it pleases my lord," said Sifka, "I only told her what chanced between King Heidrek and your son at the hunt yesterday. Heidrek has slain the boy; when the queen heard the news, it grieved her, and so she fled the hall, weeping."

The king of the Gardar became very angry. He called for his men to seize Heidrek. "Take that man prisoner!" he commanded. "Throw him in shackles that he might answer for his crimes!"

The king's men sat in silent puzzlement. They all liked Heidrek very much and could see no reason why he should be put into chains. Then two men stood forth and said, "We will do this thing, my lord," and they seized Heidrek, bound him, and made him stand before the king of the Gardar. These two men were the ones that Heidrek had ransomed from their bonds many years ago.

Heidrek, meanwhile, sent one of his men to fetch the young prince while the king of the Gardar summoned his court to hear the charges against Heidrek. The king told the people what Sifka had told him, that Heidrek had killed his son. Then the king said, "For this foul deed, Heidrek, I command that you hang by the neck until dead, like the murderous dog that you are."

Just as the king pronounced his sentence, the young boy came running into the court. "Father!" he cried. "Please don't kill him! I am alive and well, and King Heidrek has done nothing to harm me. He has been the best of foster-fathers, and you have no reason to hurt him at all."

Heidrek was released from his bonds and immediately made ready to depart. The queen of the Gardar saw that Heidrek was still very angry about what had happened, so she went to the king and said, "It is shameful to allow Heidrek to depart without some recompense. Offer him something in redress, and be reconciled to him."

The king agreed that the queen's advice was good, so he went to Heidrek and said, "I would that we might be friends again. I wish to give recompense for the shame you suffered at my hands. I have a great store of gold and would willingly part with every coin of it to redress your hurt."

"I have gold enough," said Heidrek. "Keep your treasure."

The king went away sad that he could not appease Heidrek. When he told the queen what had passed, the queen said, "If he will not take gold, then offer him your best liegemen and a share of your realm. Surely he will not be able to refuse such a gift."

The king went to Heidrek and said, "If you will not take my gold, then take my best liegemen to be your own and as large a share of my realm as you care to have. I give all to you very willingly to mend the hurt I have caused."

Heidrek said, "I have men enough, and my dominion is already very large. I will not take any of that from you."

Again, the king went away sad that Heidrek would not take what was offered. He told the queen what had happened, and she said, "If he will take neither gold, nor men, nor lands, then give him your most precious possession. Offer him your daughter's hand."

"I had hoped that would not be necessary, but I now see the wisdom in that. I shall do as you suggest."

The king went to Heidrek and said, "If you will take neither treasure, nor men, nor lands, then perhaps you will consent to wed my daughter? I have nothing more precious, and it pains me that we should part without reconciling."

Heidrek accepted this gift and so made peace with the king of the Gardar.

When Heidrek returned home, he decided that he needed to be rid of Sifka. He summoned her and said, "Make ready to leave. We go on a journey together."

Sifka did as she was told. She met Heidrek in the courtyard, where Heidrek's best horse stood saddled. Heidrek put Sifka on this animal, then took the reins and led it away from his stronghold. They walked for a very long way, until the horse finally became so exhausted that it fell down and would not rise. Heidrek left the horse where it was and commanded Sifka to walk. They went on until they came to a river that was both wide and deep. Sifka said, "How am I to cross such a river? I have not the strength to do this."

Heidrek said, "Climb up on my shoulders, and I will carry you across."

Sifka did so, but in the middle of the stream, Heidrek tossed her off his shoulders. He grabbed her body and broke her spine, then dumped her into the river, where she floated away with the current, dead. Then Heidrek returned home and commanded a great wedding feast to be held. He married the daughter of the king of the Gardar. Together they had a daughter named Hervor. She was fostered in England by Earl Frodmar and became a shieldmaiden, and she was as doughty as the strongest warrior.

Of Heidrek and the Riddle-Contest

Heidrek had now become a very wealthy lord and the king of a wide realm. All the lords of the lands around respected him, and many paid him tribute. Having finished his days of conquest, Heidrek set about putting order in his kingdom. He declared that all disputes would be heard by a group of twelve judges chosen from among the wisest men of the land, and that their word should decide the cases brought before them. Heidrek also bred a special boar that he dedicated to the god Frey. The boar was nearly as large as a full-grown ox, and its coat was made of the softest, finest hair that shone in the sun like gold.

Now, it became the custom for all the men of Heidrek's court to gather at a feast on the eve of Yuletide, and at this feast, they would make their vows for the coming year. But instead of drinking the pledge cup, they would place one hand on the golden boar's head and another on his back and so make their vows, swearing by the great animal beneath their hands. One Yuletide Eve, the men took their turns swearing their oaths on the great boar, and when Heidrek's turn came, he said, "This I swear by Frey's golden boar: that whosoever shall go before the twelve judges and have his case go against him, that man will receive his freedom if he comes before me and bests me in a contest of riddles."

It came to pass that a man named Gestumblindi fell afoul of Heidrek, who summoned him to answer before the twelve judges. Gestumblindi knew that the judgment was likely to go against him, so he offered many sacrifices to Odin, praying that he might be delivered from his fate. On the evening before the trial, Gestumblindi sat staring into the fire, worrying about what might chance in the morning. He sighed and stood up from his chair, thinking that he might as well go and sleep. When he turned away from the fire, he saw a man standing before him. The man was dressed in rough traveler's clothes and a wide-brimmed hat. He had a mighty spear in one hand and a patch over one eye. This was none other than Odin himself, who had heard Gestumblindi's prayer.

"Peace, Gestumblindi," Odin said. "Be not afraid, for I have received your sacrifices and have come to help you. This is what you shall do: On the morrow you shall not go to the trial. You shall remain here at home. Hide yourself, and let no one see you, for I shall take your shape and go in your stead, and all will be well." Then Odin vanished, leaving a trembling and grateful Gestumblindi standing in an empty hall.

In the morning, Odin took on Gestumblindi's shape and went to the trial. The judges heard the evidence and decided against Gestumblindi. "You have heard the judgment," said the king. "Will you take your punishment, or will you face me in a contest of riddles?"

"I know you to be a crafty and cunning man," said Gestumblindi. "I fear that whatever I do, the end will be the same for me."

"Be that as it may," said the king, "you still must decide here and now which path you will take."

"Very well," said Gestumblindi. "I will play at riddles with you."

"Good," said the king. "Ask me a riddle, and if I cannot answer it, you will go free. If I answer all your riddles, the punishment stands."

"Here is my first riddle," said Gestumblindi.

I left my house and went on a journey.

I journeyed over a road made of roads.

There was a road above me

And a road beneath me

And roads on every side of me.

What is the answer to my riddle?

"Ah, that is an easy one," said the king. "You crossed a bridge, and there were birds flying above you and to the side of you. The bridge went over a river that had fish swimming in it. Tell me another."

Gestumblindi said,

Yesterday when I awoke, I drank a drink

that was not wine, nor was it ale,

and I neither drank mead nor ate food,

yet I slaked my thirst.

What is the answer to my riddle?

"This is a good one," said the king, "but I know the answer. You lay on the grass, and when you woke, you lapped up the dew that had fallen. Tell me another."

Gestumblindi said,

Who is it that shrieks
as he walks on hard paths
that he treads over and over?
Two mouths he has
and is always kissing,
and the path he treads is made of gold.

"This one is obvious," said Heidrek. "It is the hammer used by a goldsmith, and its shrieks are the sounds made when it strikes the anvil. Have you no better riddles?"

Gestumblindi said,

I pass over the ground
swallowing forest and field as I go;
I flee before no man
but I run when the wind blows,
and always I battle with the sun.

"That is fog," said Heidrek. "It enwraps and enshrouds everything and blots out the sun, but the wind can blow it away. Do you have another riddle?"

Gestumblindi said,

Maidens are we,
running all together
as our father chases us.
Our hair is pale
and our hoods are white,
and no man shall ever know us.

"I know this one," said Heidrek. "Those are waves. Tell me another."

Gestumblindi said,

Four I have that dangle down,

Four I have that tread the ground.

To show the way out I have two

and also, to keep away dogs.

A filthy one dangles behind me.

"Ha!" cried Heidrek. "That is easy. It is a cow. Have you no better riddles?"

Gestumblindi said,

I am two that runs

with ten feet and three eyes

and I have but one tail.

"That is Odin when he rides upon Sleipnir," said Heidrek. "Make your next riddle more difficult."

"This riddle will be my last, and you will know the answer only if you are truly the wisest of all kings," said Gestumblindi. "Here is my riddle: What did Odin whisper in Baldur's ear before kindling his pyre?"

"Who else but you would know the answer?" cried Heidrek as he drew his sword and slashed at Odin. But Odin turned himself into a hawk and flew away, and the blow only severed the end of his tail feathers. This is why hawks have short tails today.

Then Odin took his own form and said, "Heidrek, you have tried to kill me without just cause, and for this I pronounce your doom: You will die a lowly death, slain not in battle by a warrior but murdered in your bed by a slave." Then Odin vanished, leaving Heidrek to ponder what he had said.

Now, some years ago, Heidrek had gone raiding and had captured nine slaves. These slaves were all noblemen, and they chafed at being held in thrall. They were always looking for ways to escape and bided their time patiently until they saw their chance.

That chance came when one-night King Heidrek went to his chamber to sleep. He had few guards, and the night was moonless and still. The slaves found themselves weapons and crept into the king's hall and then down the corridor to where the king slept. They killed the guards and went into Heidrek's chamber, where they slew him in his bed. Thus, perished King Heidrek the Wise.

In the morning, Angantyr, the king's son, called a great council where he announced the death of King Heidrek. The nobles one and all declared that Angantyr should be the king of the realm, and Angantyr accepted. "However," he said, "the murderers of my father still run free. I shall not assume the throne until I have found them and have avenged my father."

Angantyr had a reason to find the slaves other than vengeance, for when the slaves slew the king, they also took Tyrfing from his bedside and carried it away with them. Angantyr was not lightly to be deprived of his birthright, and so he went in search of the slaves meaning to kill them all and take Tyrfing back.

One evening, Angantyr found himself walking along the mouth of the river Grafa, where he saw three men in a boat, fishing. As Angantyr watched, one of the men caught a fish on his line and landed it in the boat.

"Pass me the bait knife, will you?" said the man who had caught the fish.

"You'll have to wait," said the other. "I'm using it right now."

Instead of waiting, the first man took a sword from the bottom of the boat. He drew the sword and used it to cut off the fish's head. Then the man said,

A pike it is who loses its head
in payment for Heidrek's death

here at Grafa-mouth

at the feet of the Harvathi Mountains.

When Angantyr heard this, he knew that the men were three of the escaped slaves and that the sword was Tyrfing. Angantyr watched as the fishermen finished their work and then rowed back to shore. He waited in the forest until night fell, and then sought out the place where the slaves had made their camp. He crept into their camp as they slept, then pulled their tent down upon them and slew them all. Then he took Tyrfing and went back to his stronghold, having avenged the death of his father.

The next episode of the saga tells of the conflict between Angantyr and his half-brother, Hlöd. Hlöd goes to Reidgotaland to demand his share of the inheritance. Angantyr makes a generous offer, although it is short of an equal division of Heidrek's lands and treasure. Gizur, Hlöd's foster-father and one of Angantyr's courtiers, thinks that less than a half share is still too great, considering that Hlöd's mother was a war captive and bondmaid. Hlöd is greatly insulted by this. He returns home and tells his grandfather, Humli, the king of the Huns, that Angantyr refused to share the inheritance equally. Humli assembles a great army to challenge Angantyr in revenge for the insult. The battle goes on for eight days. On the last day, Angantyr kills both Hlöd and Humli, much to his sorrow, and the Gothic warriors rout the Hunnish army.

The final portion of the saga is a concise history of the kings of Sweden from Angantyr's grandson, Ivar the Wide-Grasping (r. c. 655–c. 695), to Filip Halstensson (r. 1105–1118).

Selections from The Saga of Örvar-Oddr

We have already met the hero Örvar-Oddr in King Heidrek's saga, where he accompanies his friend and blood brother Hjalmar to a battle to determine whether Hjalmar is fit to wed the daughter of King Yngvi In addition to guest appearances in other sagas, Oddr is also the subject of a saga of his own, which tells of his birth and childhood, his travels to far-flung places such as Ireland and Permia (an area around the Kama River in what is now Russia), his battles with Vikings and giants, and of how he marries and becomes a king.

Örvar-Oddr's name literally translated is "Arrow's Point." (Other versions of the name in modern sources are Arrow-Odd and Orvar-Odds.) His given name is Oddr ("Point"), but the rest of the moniker was added by a giant who saw some magic arrows that Oddr had in his quiver and dubbed him "Örvar-Oddr." Unlike many ancient heroes, Oddr has two human parents and a relatively normal birth, but when he grows up, he has a hero's strength and skill and has his family's uncanny ability to get the wind to rise merely by hoisting a sail. Oddr also is headstrong and irreverent, a trickster at one moment and a fearsome warrior the next.

As is proper for such a hero, Oddr is the subject of a prophecy about the manner of his death: A venomous serpent hiding inside the skull of a horse named Faxi will bite him. Oddr takes measures to defeat the prophecy, but no man can defy fate. When Oddr returns to Berurjod, where he was fostered, he prods the skull of a horse that he finds lying on the beach, and as predicted, a venomous serpent strikes from underneath, and Oddr dies from the serpent's venom.

Oddr's saga is too long to present in its entirety in this book, and so only a select few episodes are retold here.

The Childhood of Örvar-Oddr

Once there was a man named Grim Hairy-Cheeks who lived in Hrafnista in Norway. Grim was the son of Ketil Trout, and he was a very wealthy and very well-respected man. Grim's wife was Lofthaena, the daughter of Harald, chieftain of Oslofjord. Lofthaena was very beautiful and quite the cleverest woman in all of Norway. Grim loved her very dearly and couldn't bear to deny her whatever she wished.

One day, Grim decided to sail to Oslofjord to attend to some business he had there. He intended to go without his wife on this particular journey because she was heavily pregnant with their first child, and he did not want anything to endanger her. But when Lofthaena heard he was leaving for Oslofjord, she demanded to go along. Grim tried to dissuade her, but Lofthaena insisted, and so Grim allowed her to come with him.

Grim fitted out two fine ships, and on the day, they were to depart, they had a fair wind. They had sailed as far as Berurjod when Lofthaena cried out. "Husband," she said, "we must put ashore right away. My pains are upon me."

Grim immediately ordered his ship to sail for land. They put ashore near the homestead of a man named Ingjald, who lived there with his wife and their young son, who was named Asmund. Grim sent messengers to Ingjald's house to ask for help, and when Ingjald heard the message, he hitched his horses to a cart and went to the beach himself to see what might be done for Lofthaena and Grim.

"Please come up to my home," Ingjald said. "We are well prepared for guests, and my wife and the other women of my household will be more than happy to help yours with her labor."

Grim and Lofthaena gratefully accepted Ingjald's invitation. They rode up to the house in his cart, and there Lofthaena was given into the care of Ingjald's wife, while Grim was shown to the high seat in Ingjald's hall to await the birth of his child. Ingjald was the most gracious of hosts; his guests lacked for nothing and were treated with great honor.

Lofthaena came through her delivery safely. Her child was a lusty boy, and all the women of the household said they had never seen a more beautiful baby. Lofthaena held her son and said, "Take him to his father so that he can get his name."

The women took the baby to Grim, who was delighted to see his new son. Grim named him Oddr and sprinkled him with water.

After three days in Ingjald's house, Lofthaena said that she was ready to resume the journey to Oslofjord. Grim went to Ingjald to let him know that they were leaving.

"Before you go," said Ingjald, "won't you honor me with a gift?"

"Most assuredly I will," said Grim. "My wife and I are in your debt for your hospitality, and I am very wealthy. How much of my money would you like to have? Whatever you ask, it will be yours."

"I don't want money," said Ingjald. "I have plenty of my own."

"That's fine," said Grim. "Ask me for something else, then."

"Give me your son to foster," said Ingjald.

"I am willing, but first I need to ask the boy's mother what she thinks," said Grim.

When Grim asked Lofthaena about allowing Ingjald to foster Oddr, Lofthaena said, "Our host honors us with that request. Let Oddr stay here as Ingjald's foster-son."

Ingjald saw his guests down to their ship for their departure. Little Oddr stayed behind at the house with Ingjald's wife. There was a fair wind, so Grim and Lofthaena sailed quickly and safely to Oslofjord, where they conducted their business. When this was completed, they sailed for home.

As they approached Berurjod, Grim said to Lofthaena, "Shall we go to Ingjald's house so that you can visit your son?"

Lofthaena answered, "There is no need. I saw him before we left, and I don't think he was sorry to see us go. Let's continue on our way home."

And so Grim and Lofthaena went back to Hrafnista, while Oddr stayed at Ingjald's house and was brought up with Ingjald's son. Ingjald raised Grim and Lofthaena's son well. He even thought more highly of Oddr than he did of his own son.

Oddr was the strongest and best-looking of any of the boys for miles around. He learned to play sports and to shoot with a bow and arrow, although he was a very serious boy and didn't play games like children usually do. As soon as Asmund and Oddr were old enough, they became blood brothers, and Asmund was with Oddr wherever he went.

Oddr was very fond of archery. He collected arrows from every arrow maker he could find, but he did not keep the arrows properly. He left them lying about everywhere so that people were forever tripping over them in the dark, or worse, sitting on their points by accident. This happened so often that people began to complain to Ingjald.

"You really must do something about that Oddr and his arrows," they said. "The situation has become quite annoying, and besides, it's dangerous."

Ingjald agreed to speak to his foster-son about this. He went to Oddr and said, "If you're not careful, you're going to have a very bad reputation very soon."

"Why is that?" said Oddr.

"You leave your arrows strewn about everywhere. People have been tripping over them and even sitting on them, and they're so tired of this that they've begun to complain about it."

"That's no fault of mine," said Oddr. "You've never made a quiver for me to put them in."

"I'd be happy to give you a fine quiver," said Ingjald. "Just tell me what you want."

"Oh, I don't think you'll be happy about this at all," said Oddr.

"I gave you my word," said Ingjald. "Ask."

"Take the black three-year-old goat that's in your herd. Kill it and skin it, but leave the horns and the hooves attached. Make me a quiver out of that hide, and mind you keep the horns and hooves as part of the quiver."

Ingjald saw to it that the quiver was made exactly as Oddr had requested. Oddr put all his arrows into it. It was a large quiver, bigger than anyone else had, and full of arrows that were longer and stronger than the arrows anyone else used. When the quiver was full, Oddr had himself a bow made to match the arrows.

Oddr liked to dress well. He had a fine red tunic that he liked to wear every day, and a gold headband that he put around his head. Everywhere he went, he took his quiver and bow with him. Oddr had one other peculiarity: He did not believe in the gods and refused to offer any sacrifices. "I'm strong enough to look after myself," he would say when people asked him about this. "I don't need a god's help to do what needs doing."

Asmund joined Oddr in this refusal, and in this they were both unlike their foster-father, who regularly offered sacrifices to Odin and the other gods. Asmund also joined Oddr in his boat, and the two of them often could be seen rowing up and down the coast together.

The Prophecy

Once there was a wise old woman named Heid. She had the gift of sight and would travel around the country telling people what their fates would be. One day, she went to visit one of Ingjald's neighbors, and Ingjald heard that she was a guest there.

Ingjald went to Asmund and Oddr and said, "I have something I need you to do for me."

"What is that?" said Oddr.

"The seeress Heid is visiting not far from here," said Ingjald. "I've prepared a feast for her. I want you to invite her here so that she can tell everyone their fates."

"Absolutely not," said Oddr. "I don't want that old witch anywhere near me. Don't you dare have her in this household."

"Very well," said Ingjald. "Asmund can do the errand alone just as well as in your company, and he's more obedient, anyway."

"Don't send Asmund by himself either," said Oddr. "If that witch comes here, I'll have to do something to show you how very displeased I am."

In the end, Asmund went by himself to invite Heid to be a guest in his father's house. Heid gladly accepted and came to Ingjald's homestead with the fifteen boys and fifteen girls that attended her everywhere she went. When Heid arrived, Ingjald came to meet her at the door with all of the men of his household. Ingjald invited Heid inside and made sure she had everything she needed for the fortune-telling, which was to be on the day after the feast. Heid and her followers feasted well with Ingjald and his household, and when the meal was done, Ingjald and his people went to bed while Heid and her followers left the house to do the rituals needed for the fortune-telling.

In the morning, Ingjald went to Heid and said, "Did your rituals go well? Are you ready to tell us our fates?"

"They went well," said Heid. "I am ready."

Ingjald gathered his household together. "Sit down, everyone. We'll go up one at a time for Heid to tell us what is in store for our futures."

As the head of the household, Ingjald went first. He stood before the old seeress, who said, "I am glad to see you here, Ingjald. Your fate is to be respected and honored by everyone for the rest of your life."

Ingjald was very pleased with this. He thanked Heid and went back to his seat.

Asmund took his turn next.

"I am glad to see you here, Asmund. You'll have a good reputation far and wide. You'll not live to a great age, but everyone will know how brave you are, and what a fine warrior."

Asmund thanked the seeress and went back to his seat. Each person in the household took their turn hearing their fate from her, and no one left disappointed. After Heid had spoken with everyone in turn, she made some prophecies about the winter to come and about many other things. Ingjald thanked her well when she was done.

"Now," said Heid, "are we sure that I've seen everyone in your household? I don't want to leave the job unfinished."

"I think so," said Ingjald.

"What's that over there on that bench?" asked Heid.

Ingjald glanced in that direction. "Oh, that's just a cloak that someone left behind."

"It's an odd cloak that twitches whenever I look at it," said Heid.

No sooner had Heid said this than the person under the cloak sat up. It was Oddr, who was furious that Ingjald had invited the seeress there against his wishes.

"Yes, this cloak twitches, because I'm right here underneath it," said Oddr. "And I'll tell you what I want from you: I want you to shut up and go away. You're not wanted here. There's nothing you can tell me about my future, so you need to leave right now."

Oddr was holding a stick, which he showed to Heid. "See this stick? I'll whack you with it if you breathe one word of prophecy about me."

"I'll not be silent," said Heid. "It's my duty to tell the fate of everyone who comes before me. Besides, you'd do very well to listen to me." Then Heid spoke this prophecy:

You fail to frighten me

Oddr, Ingjald's foster-son.

Your stick is not stronger

than my seeing,

and always I speak true.

Run and roam as you might,

on wave, on shore,

fate always finds a man

no matter where he goes.

Bound you shall be

by your destiny

to die here at Berurjod.

From the skull of Faxi

the sly serpent will strike.

Venomous fangs

will find your heel,

dealing out death to you after you have lived a long life.

Then the seeress said, "I have this also to tell you: Your life will be many times that of other men. Three hundred years will you wander the world, and everywhere you go you will conquer. But it won't matter how well you fight or how well everyone esteems you; the skull of the horse Faxi will be your doom, right here in Berurjod. There is no way you can escape your fate."

"Shut up, witch!" cried Oddr. "I told you not to say anything at all about me!"

Then Oddr hit the seeress in the face with his stick, breaking her nose and covering her face with blood.

"I'll not stay here a moment longer," said the seeress. "Get my belongings. I'm leaving. Never have I ever been treated this way in a place where I made prophecies."

"Please don't leave," said Ingjald. "Allow me to recompense you. I have many valuable gifts to give you if you stay here for three more nights."

"The gifts I'll take in redress for my injury," said the seeress, "but I'll not stay a moment longer."

As soon as Ingjald had given the old woman the gifts he had promised, she left his house and never came back.

When the seeress had gone, Oddr went to Asmund and said, "Come with me. We have a job to do."

Oddr and Asmund went to the stables, where they found the horse named Faxi. They bridled the horse and then led it away from the house and into the woods. They found the place that Oddr was seeking, and there they tied the horse up while the two of them dug a deep pit. By the time they were done digging, the lip of the pit was many feet above their heads. Once Oddr was satisfied that the pit was deep enough, they killed Faxi and pushed his body into the pit. Then

Oddr and Asmund gathered many large stones and pushed them into the pit on top of the horse's body. Over each layer of stones, they poured a layer of sand to seal up the cracks between the stones, and they did not stop until they had raised a large mound over the horse's grave.

When the work was done, Oddr looked at the mound of stones and smirked. "Let's see whether Faxi's skull can manage to get out of that," he said. "That'll teach that old witch to make prophecies about me. There's no way anything she said is going to come true."

Oddr and Asmund returned to the house, where they went to speak to Ingjald. Oddr said to Ingjald, "Give me some ships."

"What for?" said Ingjald. "What are you planning to do with them?"

"I'm leaving," said Oddr. "I'm leaving, and I'm never coming back."

"Please don't go," said Ingjald. "I can't bear to see you leave."

"You can't sway me," said Oddr. "I'll not stay any longer."

"You can't sail a ship by yourself," said Ingjald. "Who will go with you? Where is your crew?"

"Asmund is coming with me," said Oddr. "We can sail just fine by ourselves."

"It's hard of you, Oddr, to leave me and take my son with you. Go away if you must, but let Asmund come back soon."

"Oh, Asmund won't come back any time before I do," said Oddr. "And besides, this serves you right for inviting that horrid old witch here when I told you I didn't want you to."

And so Ingjald gave Oddr and Asmund one of his ships, and when they had prepared for their voyage, he went down to the beach to see them off.

"Good luck to you," said Ingjald. "Good luck and a safe voyage. Maybe someday I will see you both again."

When Oddr and Asmund had said their own farewells to Ingjald, they pushed their ship out into the surf and rowed away. Ingjald watched them until they had rowed out of sight, and then he went back to his house.

Örvar-Oddr in the Land of the Giants

One day, Oddr was traveling about and came to a steep cliff that overlooked a gorge. In the gorge was a river that was roaring along in cascading rapids. Oddr needed to get to the other side of the gorge, but he could see no way across. He decided to have a rest to think about what to do next. He had hardly sat down when something very large and very strong grabbed him about the shoulders and lifted him off the ground. A giant vulture had swooped down and snatched Oddr up in its talons, and now it was flying away with him.

The vulture flew a very long way. It sailed over the gorge and over the lands beyond. It sailed on across the sea until it came to an island that rose out of the sea in sheer cliffs. On a shelf of rock on the cliffside was the vulture's nest, and in the nest were several hungry chicks. The vulture dropped Oddr into the nest amongst the chicks, but Oddr remained unharmed because he was wearing his magic shirt that protected him from all injuries.

Now Oddr was in an even worse plight than he had been at the cliff's edge, for here the cliffs were absolutely sheer both above and below, and there was no way for him to climb out of his predicament. He looked over the edge of the nest and saw the sea churning below. For a moment, he thought about jumping from the nest into the water, but then thought better of it because the water was so very far away, and he had no idea in which direction he should swim to get to land or even how far away land might be. Oddr decided that for the moment he would conceal himself in a crevice near the nest and wait for an opportunity to escape.

Every day, the vulture flew away from the nest and came back with some sort of meat in its talons with which to feed its young. It brought every sort of animal and fish, and sometimes even human remains, which the chicks gobbled up greedily. Sometimes the vulture brought back cooked meat, which Oddr snatched away and ate himself.

One day, just after the vulture had dropped off several large, roasted oxen for its chicks to eat, Oddr saw a boat row up to the edge of the cliff. In the boat was a giant. The giant looked up to the place where the vulture's nest was and said, "There it is. That's the nest of that foul bird who keeps stealing my dinner. I had intended to feast well myself on the king's oxen, not provide a feast for others. Now I only need to figure out how to rid myself of this pest."

When Oddr heard the giant, he came out of his hiding place, killed all the chicks, and then stood up. He shouted down to the giant, "All your things are up here. I've been guarding them for you." Then he went back into the crevice to see what would happen.

The giant climbed up the side of the cliff, took the roasted oxen from the nest, and brought them down to his boat. Then he climbed back up to the nest and said, "Oi, little man! Where are you? Come out and talk to me. Don't be frightened; I'll take you away from this place."

Oddr came out of the crevice. The giant picked him up and then climbed back down the cliff and put Oddr into his boat.

The giant said to Oddr, "So, little friend, how do you think I should rid myself of that pest?"

"Set fire to the nest," said Oddr. "When the vulture returns and flies in close to see what is going on, its feathers will catch fire. That will weaken the brute, and then we can kill it."

And so Oddr and the giant put that plan into action. It didn't take long for the nest to start burning, and soon the vulture returned, just as Oddr expected it would. It flew too close to the flames, setting its feathers alight. Then Oddr swooped in and killed the vulture. When the creature was dead, Oddr cut off its beak and talons. He gave them to the giant, and then the giant carried Oddr back into his boat.

As the giant rowed away from the cliff, Oddr said, "What is your name?"

"I am called Hildir," said the giant. "I live in the Land of the Giants. My wife's name is Hildirid, and we have a daughter named Hildigunn. Just yesterday, my wife gave birth to a fine son, and we've named him Godmund. I have two brothers, named Ulf and Ylfing. We're getting ready to have a contest amongst ourselves to see which of us should be the king of the giants."

"How will the contest be decided?" said Oddr.

"Well, the one who has done the most heroic deed and whose dog wins the dogfight at the Assembly of Giants will be made king."

"Which of you do you think will win?" said Oddr.

"It won't be me, I can tell you that," said Hildir. "I've always lived in my brothers' shadows, and I don't expect that to change anytime soon."

"If you could win, would you want to be the king?" asked Oddr.

"Oh, yes, indeed, I'd love to be king," said Hildir, "but there's no way that will happen. Ulf is sure to enter his pet wolf into the dogfight, and it's never lost a fight yet; it's that strong and that savage. Ulf also went on a journey to a faraway land and brought back the head of a great catlike thing, with orange fur and black stripes. He says it's called a tiger, and that it's very fierce indeed."

"Ulf does sound like a tough competitor," said Oddr.

"Oh, Ulf is nothing to Ylfing," said the giant. "Ylfing's polar bear will make mincemeat of anything anyone cares to match it with in the dogfight, and Ylfing killed a unicorn the other day and brought back its head as evidence. I haven't done anything nearly as heroic. For that matter, I don't even own a dog."

"Yes, those do seem very difficult odds," said Oddr, "but maybe if a friend helped you, you could find a way around the problem."

The giant laughed. "Oh, you're a funny one, you are, although there's no denying you have good brains in that tiny head of yours. I think I'll give you as a present to Hildigunn. You'll make a fine toy for her, and she can take care of you and baby Godmund at the same time."

It took hardly any time for the giant to row his boat back to his home. When they arrived, Hildir showed Oddr to his daughter and said, "This little man is yours to play with. But mind you, you must treat him well! Treat him just as well as you would your baby brother."

Oddr looked up at Hildigunn. She was far from fully grown, but Oddr only came up to just above her knee, even though he was a very tall man indeed, and Hildigunn's father towered over her. Hildigunn picked up Oddr and began to dandle him on her knee. She sang:

Little tiny man with down on your chin,

Baby Godmund is already bigger than you.

Then Hildigunn took Oddr and lay him down in the cradle next to baby Godmund, and Oddr saw that he was indeed smaller even than the baby giant. For a little while, Hildigunn rocked the cradle and sang lullabies to Oddr and the baby, but eventually she decided that Oddr wasn't to sleep with Godmund but with her, so she picked Oddr up and placed him in her bed, where she hugged and kissed him all night. Oddr decided that the best strategy would be to play along with the giant girl and to wait for his chance to get away.

After a few days of playing whatever games Hildigunn asked him to play, Oddr said, "I know I seem very small indeed to you and that you think of me as a child, but among my own people, I am a grown man and am considered particularly large and strong. In fact, my people are a lot bigger and stronger than the other people who live near us, and we're better looking, too. But for all that, we're not any smarter than the other people are."

Now, the giant had rescued Oddr toward the end of the summer, and so Oddr stayed that winter with the giant family. When spring came, Oddr went to Hildir and said, "I know your assembly is coming up soon. What would you give me if I could find you a dog that could best all the other dogs at the fight there?"

"If someone could give me a dog that would win that fight, I'd give that person just about anything they asked for. Do you know where I might find such a dog?"

"I certainly do," said Oddr. "Do you know where the Vargey Islands are?"

"Yes, I know them, although I've never actually been there," said Hildir.

"Well, on those islands, there is a great creature called the brown bear. In the winter, it digs itself a den and sleeps and sleeps until spring. When spring comes, it comes out of its den and goes looking for food because it is quite famished after not having eaten for so long, and because it's so hungry, it's also very fierce and will kill and eat anything that crosses its path. It's not afraid of people at all; bears like that who live near farms will go right into the cattle pens, take a calf, and then run away with it to eat it in the forest. And if the farmer dares to get in the bear's way, well, the bear thinks that fresh farmer makes just as good a meal as fresh calf does. I think if you could find one of these bears, it probably would beat your brothers' dogs quite handily."

Hildir said, "Your story intrigues me. Tomorrow, I want you to help me catch one of these bears, and if I become king, I will reward you as generously as I can."

In the morning, as Hildir and Oddr were loading the giant's boat with supplies for their journey, Hildigunn came down to the beach and asked Oddr to step aside and have a word with her.

"Will you be coming back here when your business is done?" she said.

"I don't know," said Oddr. "But I think it rather unlikely."

"Oh, dear," said Hildigunn. "I do so wish you would come back. I love you so very much, despite your small stature. Also, you should know that I am expecting a child. There's no one else but you who could be the father, even though you're so small that one would think it impossible. But because I love you so much, I'll let you go wherever you want to go if that's what you want, but you should know that if I wanted to keep you here by force, I could most certainly do it. Instead, I'll just mourn your departure, because it's more important that you be happy than it is for you to stay here with me, and it seems to me that you don't want to stay. Now tell me, when the child is born, what shall I do with it?"

"If the child is a boy," said Oddr, "keep him with you until he is ten years old and then send him to me to be trained in the ways of men. But if the child is a girl, keep her here with you always and raise her yourself. I know you will do that very well, but I have no idea how to raise a girl myself."

Then Hildigunn said farewell to Oddr and went into the house, weeping bitterly. Oddr got into the boat, and the giant rowed them away from the shore.

Now, the giant was very strong and a very good rower, but even with calm seas, they were not making very fast progress. Oddr then decided he would use the luck of the men of Hrafnista to make their voyage go more swiftly. He hoisted a sail, and immediately a fair wind blew up. The ship leapt through the water, going twice as fast as it had been going with the giant at the oars.

The wind whipped up great waves that pitched the boat up and down. Hildir looked at the waves, and then he looked toward the shore, where it seemed that the land was jumping up and down of its own accord, which frightened Hildir greatly. Clinging to the gunwale for dear life, he went to where Oddr was standing, picked him up, and then slammed him down to the deck, pinning him there.

"I don't know how you're doing this thing," roared the giant, "but whatever witchcraft it is that makes the land jump about, stop it at once, or I will kill you and throw your carcass overboard for the fish to eat."

"What, have you never sailed before?" said Oddr. "This isn't witchcraft; it's just sailing. If you let me up, I can show you."

Hildir let Oddr stand up. Oddr lowered the sail, and immediately everything was calm.

"See?" said Oddr. "Now that we're not sailing with the wind, everything is calm. If we sail, we'll get to our destination faster, but there will be waves, and it will look like the land is jumping. You needn't worry, though; that's just what things look like when you sail. Can we try it again? We can always stop if it frightens you or if you need a rest."

Hildir agreed to let Oddr hoist the sail again now that he understood what was happening. He had also seen how much faster they had been traveling when the sail was up, and he was eager to get to the islands to catch a bear. Once the sail was up again, Hildir sat quietly near the boat's prow and let Oddr do all the work, and in no time they had arrived at the island where they were to look for a bear.

Not far from the beach was a mountain. At the base of the mountain was a great pile of scree. Oddr said, "I'll bet there's a bear in there under that scree. They like to make their dens in such places. Maybe you could put your hand in there to see what you'll find."

"That's a good idea," said Hildir, who pushed his great hand into the stones and began feeling about. When he had pushed his whole arm in right up to his shoulder, he stopped and said, "I think there's something here that might be a bear. I'm going to put on a glove before I try to grab it, though."

Hildir put on his glove and plunged his arm back into the scree. When he brought his arm back out, he was pulling a bear along by its ears. The bear was very angry at having been pulled out of its den early. It scratched and bit, and soon Hildir's hands were covered with cuts.

"You were right about how fierce this beast is," said Hildir. "What do I do now?"

"Take the bear home with you, and put it somewhere safe inside your house where no one can see it and where it can't get out. Don't feed it anything until after the dogfight. When it's time for your assembly, pit your bear against your brothers' dogs. If your bear doesn't win, then meet me back here at the same time next year so that I can give you something else to try."

"I'd like you to meet me here at this same spot next year whatever happens at the assembly," said the giant.

"Very well," said Oddr. "I will be here."

Then Hildir and Oddr said their farewells. Hildir set off for home in his boat with the bear, and Oddr went his own way.

As he had promised, Oddr returned to that place the following spring. He went a little way into the forest that was nearby, thinking that Hildir might want to kill him if the bear hadn't won the contest as Oddr said it would. Oddr didn't have long to wait before Hildir drew his boat up onto the beach. The giant took two chests and a great cauldron full of silver out of the boat and set them down in the place where he had promised to meet Oddr. Hildir waited for a while, but Oddr did not show himself. Hildir waited a little while more, then sighed and said, "Oddr, I do so wish you were here to take your reward. It's really not polite for you not to meet me here when you said you would. But I can't stay any longer. I can't leave my kingdom unguarded. Here are two chests filled with gold and a cauldron filled with silver. I'll put this big stone on top of them so that the wind can't take them away, and I'll put some other treasures here on top of the stone.

"Maybe you are waiting nearby and don't want to show yourself, so in case you can hear me: My dog bested all the others at the assembly, and when the people saw the beak and talons of that foul vulture that we killed last year, they decided I was the most valiant of all my brothers. I've been made king, and I've you to thank for it. If you ever decide to come and visit me, I'll treat you as a most honored guest. And I'd also like to let you know that Hildigunn had her baby. He's a fine boy, and we've named him Vignir. Hildigunn says that you're the father, but I'll raise him like he's my very own. I'll teach him all the things a boy should know, and when he's ten years old, we'll send him to you, as Hildigunn promised she would do."

Then the giant got back into his boat and rowed away. Oddr came out of his hiding place and saw that the giant had placed a sword, a helmet, and a shield on top of the stone. Oddr took those things off the great slab and then tried to push the stone aside, but it was so heavy that even with many strong men to help him, he would not be able to lift it. So Oddr took the weapons that the giant had left and felt very well recompensed indeed, for these were all very valuable treasures.

The Voyages to Vinland

The story of the attempted Viking settlement in what is now eastern Canada was the subject of much controversy for a very long time. Many scholars had doubted its historical veracity, but in 1960, the Norwegian archaeologist Anne Stine Ingstad and her husband Helge discovered the remains of what seemed to be a Viking settlement in L'Anse aux Meadows on the large island on the Gulf of St Lawrence in Newfoundland. At this site, which apparently was in use c. 990-1050 CE, Ingstad found the remains of several houses, everyday household items, the remains of a loom, an iron smithy, and rivets such as those that Vikings used to build their ships. While it is unlikely that this particular settlement is the one called "Leif's houses" in the saga, it provides incontrovertible proof of a Norse presence in North America around the turn of the eleventh century. Not only that, but more recent archaeological excavations, such as the one on Baffin Island in the Canadian province of Nunavut that began in 2001, have continued to turn up evidence of other Viking settlements.

The Vinland Sagas is the collective title given to The Saga of Eirik the Red *and* The Saga of the Greenlanders, *each of which contain a version of the Norse sojourns in northeastern Canada. Although it is now generally accepted that Norse explorers did make relatively short-lived settlements in North America, it would be a mistake to take these thirteenth-century Norse texts as actual historical documents, not least because they contain elements that suggest a certain amount of romanticization of this new place the Norse called "Vinland," supposedly named after the great number of wild grapes that grew there. One such romanticized element concerns the harshness of the winters. The sagas report that the winters at the Vinland settlement were relatively mild, without much snow or freezing temperatures, but anyone who knows anything about northeastern Canadian weather will understand this to be more a product of wishful thinking (or perhaps an element of propaganda) than a description of actual winter conditions in that part of the world.*

Despite their fictionalization of historical events, The Vinland Sagas *remain vital documents in the history of both Europe and the Americas. In these sagas, we read of the first attempted European settlements in North America and the first contacts between Europeans and Indigenous Americans, and of the courage and resourcefulness of the Norse people who made voyages west to explore a new land.*

Of Bjarni Herjolfsson

Once there was a man named Bjarni Herjolfsson who was a well-respected merchant with his own ship. Bjarni's parents lived in Iceland. Sometimes Bjarni would spend his winters with them, while at other times he would spend them in Norway. Bjarni was an adventurous man, well willing to take risks to find new lands.

One summer, Bjarni's father, Herjolf, decided to leave Iceland and join Eirik the Red's new settlement in Greenland. Herjolf sold his farm, then put his family, slaves, and possessions into ships and sailed to Greenland, where he began a new farm at a place he called Herjolfsness. As he had been in Iceland, Herjolf was a well-respected and well-off man in Greenland as well.

Now, Herjolf moved to Greenland while Bjarni was away on a voyage. When Bjarni arrived at the port in Iceland, he went up to his father's farm to visit his parents, but he found the farmstead abandoned. Alarmed, Bjarni rushed over to a neighbor's house and asked what had become of his family. "Oh, they up and moved to Greenland, they did," said the neighbor. "Went to join old Eirik at that new colony of his."

Bjarni was pleased to find that nothing terrible had happened to his family in his absence, but now he had to decide whether to winter in Iceland or to go elsewhere. As he walked back to the port, he decided he would go and find his family and winter with them, as had been his custom on occasion. Bjarni arrived back at the ship, where his men had started unloading their cargo.

Bjarni said, "Stop unloading. We need to discuss what we're going to do. My father has moved to Greenland, so I'd like to go there to trade our goods and spend the winter. Who will come with me?"

The sailors all agreed that they'd go with Bjarni, even though none of them had ever sailed to Greenland before and only knew which direction to sail, but not exactly where Greenland lay.

As soon as the tide turned, Bjarni and his men sailed away from Iceland with a good, fair wind. They sailed for three days with this wind, and at the end of the third day, they were on the open ocean with no land in sight. It was then that their fortunes turned. The wind that had taken them this far shifted to the north, and thick fog descended all around them. They struck their sails to wait for the fog to dissipate, not wanting to lose their way at a time when the winds were against them and they could see nothing but the patch of sea on which their ship was bobbing.

Finally, the fog cleared, and the men were able to get their bearings. The wind was fair once more, so they hoisted the sail and continued their journey. After another day's sailing, they sighted land.

"Is this Greenland?" asked one of the sailors.

"I'm not sure," said Bjarni, "but I don't think it is. I don't know where we are."

"What shall we do now?" asked another sailor.

"Let's sail closer to that land and see what manner of place it is. Perhaps I am mistaken and it is Greenland indeed."

When the ship neared the coastline, Bjarni saw that they were in a strange land that neither he nor his men had ever seen before. Bjarni had heard people tell of Greenland, that it had many mountains and cliffs and glaciers, but this new land was nothing like that. The land was covered with thick forests that blanketed softly rolling hills, and there was no ice to be seen anywhere. Bjarni's ship had come fairly close to land when the wind failed.

"I say we put in here and take on firewood and water," said one sailor. "We don't know where we are, and who knows when we'll next have that chance?"

"No," said Bjarni. "We sail on. We have wood and water aplenty. We'll sail close to this coastline, and if need be, we can beach the ship farther on."

"This is folly," said one of the sailors. "We'll end up in the middle of the ocean with nothing to drink."

"Yes," said another. "We should put in here. It won't take us long, and we'll be glad we did later."

The other sailors agreed that this was the best plan, but Bjarni overruled them, and so they sailed on along this strange, new coastline. After a time, they came to a new place that was mountainous and covered with glaciers.

"Is this Greenland?" asked one of the sailors.

"I don't think so," said Bjarni. "From what I've heard, Greenland is a much more hospitable place than this. Let's sail on."

And so they sailed, hugging this new coastline, and soon they discovered that this place was a small island and not Greenland at all. They changed their course to leave the island behind them, setting out in the direction they thought best and with a good, fair wind.

Toward the end of the day, clouds rolled in, and a great storm began to blow around them. "Reef the sail!" said Bjarni. "Make sure the cargo is secure! We'll run before the storm, but I'll not have us lose our sail and rigging!"

It was a hard time and a dangerous one. The little ship was tossed on the waves, and the sail and rigging strained under the force of the wind. For four days the storm blew, but when it finally cleared, Bjarni and his men saw land on the horizon.

"Is this Greenland?" asked the sailors.

"I think it might be," said Bjarni, "but we'll need to sail closer."

They sailed on, and when they were close enough to see the features of the land, Bjarni said, "Yes, I think this is Greenland. This is the kind of place others have told me about. We'll beach the ship here. At the very least, we need to rest and take on water and other supplies before we go any farther."

As the ship approached the shore, they saw that another ship was already beached there before them. "This is a good sign," said Bjarni. "At the very least, we've come to a place where others make their homes. They'll be able to tell us where we are."

They beached the ship, and then Bjarni said, "I'm going to go in search of whoever lives here. Two of you come with me, and the rest stay here and see to repairs."

Bjarni and his companions walked inland, and soon they came to a prosperous farmstead. They knocked on the door of the farmhouse, and who should answer but Bjarni's own father!

"Bjarni! Welcome, my boy, and welcome to your friends!" said Bjarni's father. "We hadn't thought to see you for another year at least. Come in, come in, and tell me and your mother how you have fared."

Bjarni was delighted to have reached Greenland at last, and he was even more delighted that the first Greenlanders he met were his very own family. Bjarni and his men took some refreshment and spoke for a while with Bjarni's parents, but they did not stay long.

"I need to go back to my ship to let my men know that we have come to a safe port and can begin trading," said Bjarni. "I'll come back as soon as my business is done and spend the winter here with you, if I may."

Bjarni's family said that he was more than welcome, and they offered to find lodgings for his men as well. Bjarni and his friends went back to their ship in high spirits, and when all their cargo had been sold and the profits fairly divided, they went their own ways to the places where they were to spend the winter.

When the spring came, Bjarni's father said, "So, my boy, are you taking to the sea again? What do you plan to do next?"

"I've had enough of voyaging," said Bjarni. "I'd like to stay here and help you with the farm, if that suits you and Mother."

"Of course!" said Bjarni's father. "You are more than welcome here. We're very glad you've come home to us."

And so it was that Bjarni gave up his life of voyaging and stayed on his father's farm. Bjarni took the farm over when Herjolf died, but he never forgot the new lands he had seen rising out of the sea, far from Greenland's shores.

Of Leif Eiriksson

One time after he had ended his trading voyages, Bjarni Herjolfsson sailed to Norway to visit Earl Eirik Hakonarson. The earl was delighted to have Bjarni as a guest, and he listened with great interest to Bjarni's tale of his adventure to the west of Greenland, but because Bjarni could not give a greater description of the country he had found, many people thought that he had lacked both courage and curiosity and thought less of him for that. For his part, the earl thought that Bjarni had done well, and made Bjarni a retainer at his court. Bjarni spent the winter in Norway with Earl Eirik and then returned to Greenland in the summer.

Word spread quickly of Bjarni's adventure. Many people wondered whether it would be possible to find those lands again and maybe even make a new settlement there. Leif, the son of Eirik the Red, heard Bjarni's tale and decided that he would try his own luck at finding that place to see whether it might be fit to settle.

Leif went to Herjolfsness to visit Bjarni. "I'd like to buy your ship," said Leif. "And I want to hear all about your adventure. I'm gathering men and supplies for a journey to that place, and it will help me if you can tell me all you know."

Bjarni readily agreed to sell his ship and tell Leif everything he could about his journey. When that business was accomplished, Leif sent word that he was seeking a crew for this adventure. He hired thirty-five men to sail with him.

When everything was ready, Leif went to his father and said, "I'm ready to leave for that new land Bjarni found. Will you come with me and help lead the expedition?"

"I'm honored to be asked, my son," said Eirik, "but I am an old man now. Sailing is a nasty, cold, wet, uncomfortable business, and I no longer have the strength for it. Your journey is a job for young men like yourself."

"Oh, come now, Father," said Leif. "You're not as old and weak as you seem. I'm sure the voyage would do you good, and it will help to have someone of your stature as part of our expedition. It will bring us luck."

In the end, Eirik agreed to join the adventure, but on the day they were to embark, Eirik was thrown from his horse on the way to the port. Eirik's leg was badly injured.

"This is a sign that I am not to go with you," said Eirik. "I should stay here. That is to be my fate."

And so Eirik went back to his homestead, and Leif commanded the journey alone.

Leif and his crew finished their preparations and set sail. It was not many days before they sighted land to the west. "This must be the land Bjarni spoke of," said Leif. "We will sail closer and then go ashore to see what may be seen."

They sailed closer to the land until they found a good place to drop their anchor. Then Leif took a party of men with him and rowed ashore. When they arrived on the land, they saw that it was mostly flat rock and glaciers. "This cannot be the land that Bjarni told us of," said Leif. "This is no place for a settlement. We'll go back to the ship and then sail on. But we have done better than Bjarni did, for we came ashore to see what we might find. Since all we found were stone and ice, I shall call this place Helluland [Stone-slab Land]."

Leif and his men returned to their ship. They set sail again, moving down the coast until they came to a different land, one that was not all rock and ice. As before, they sailed close to the shore and dropped their anchor. Leif chose a party of men to go ashore with him. They rowed onto the beach, which was made of fine white sand. Leif and his men walked inland. They found that the land was relatively flat and had many dense forests. "We will call this place Markland [Forest Land]," said Leif. "But we won't stay here. Let's sail on and see what else we might find."

Leif and his crew sailed for two days before they sighted another shore. This time, they had arrived at an island. They went ashore and walked through the dewy grass. The men collected the dew in their hands and tasted it.

"This is so good!" said one man.

"Yes!" said another. "Even at home the dew is not as sweet."

They explored the island for a while longer, then returned to their ship and sailed around the island, which was not far from a much greater land. They sailed into the sound between the island and the headland that lay to their north, then rounded the headland. There they met with their first real difficulty: The water here was very shallow, and so when the tide lowered, the ship was left stranded on the sand.

"I don't want to wait here," said Leif. "We should go ashore anyway. We have plenty of time before the tide changes and we can sail once more."

Leif and his men walked to the shore, bringing rowboats with them. There they found a river that flowed to the sea, and by following the river, they soon came to a lake.

"This is a good place," said Leif. "Let's go back to the ship. When the tide lifts it, we can row upriver and drop anchor in the lake."

As soon as the water was deep enough, Leif and his crew rowed their ship up the river and into the lake, where they dropped their anchor. They took their bedrolls and other supplies to the shore, where they built shelters out of stone and turf. They took their fishing gear and caught many fine salmon, which were plentiful both in the lake and in the river.

"Look at this beast!" said one man, holding up a huge salmon he had just caught. "Have you ever seen its like? Even at home we have no such salmon as this. Tonight, we eat well!"

It wasn't long until Leif and his men decided that they would spend the winter there to see what it was like. They built proper houses for themselves since the shelters would not be sufficient for the colder weather.

When winter came, the explorers were pleased to find that it was much less cold than at home, and the grass was still good for cattle to graze. Although the nights lengthened and the days shortened as the solstice approached, the sun still rose and was in the sky for part of the day, unlike at home, where both days and nights were dark at that time.

Once the houses were built, Leif explained how they were to go about exploring the land. "Every day, we will split up into two groups. One group stays here with the houses. The other group goes exploring. But the explorers must be able to return to the houses before sunset, and no one must leave the group for any reason."

This was how they lived for some time. On some days, Leif would stay with the houses, while on other days he went with the explorers. One day, Leif stayed at the houses, while the others went out to scout the land. The exploration party returned to the houses, but one of the explorers was missing, a German man by the name of Tyrkir, who was a great friend of Eirik the Red's and who had been Leif's foster-father when he was a boy.

"Where is Tyrkir?" Leif demanded of the explorers. "You knew you weren't supposed to let anyone separate from the group. I need to be able to trust all of you to follow orders, and this day you have not."

Leif then chose twelve men to accompany him to look for Tyrkir, but they had not gone far before Tyrkir appeared.

"Tyrkir!" Leif shouted. "Thank the gods you are safe. Where have you been?"

Tyrkir replied with a flood of rapid German that none of the others understood. The older man seemed very excited about something, hardly able to contain himself.

"Slow down, foster-father," said Leif. "Slow down, and speak Norse. We don't understand you at all."

Tyrkir took a deep breath, then replied in Norse. "Grapes! Grapes and grapevines! Whole fields of them!"

"Are you sure?" said Leif.

"Very sure," said Tyrkir. "Where I come from, they grow many grapes. I know what grapes and grapevines look like. Come, I'll show you."

Leif saw that the shadows were lengthening and that night was not far off. "No, we'll not go now," he said. "It's too close to nightfall. Let's go back to the houses and have a meal. We'll go to the grapevines in the morning."

When the sun rose, Leif gathered all the men together. "Here is what we will do. We will cut grapes and grapevines to take home, and also a load of timber. Then we'll go back to Greenland and tell everyone what we have found in this new place. We will call it Vinland [Wine Land] since it has such an abundance of grapes and grapevines."

The men agreed that this was the best course to take, and so they began doing the work that Leif had suggested they do.

When spring came, they made everything ready to sail home. The ship was laden with grapes, vines, and timber, and the men were well pleased with what they had found. They had a fair wind and a sunny day when they departed Vinland, and everyone was in high spirits.

They sailed on for a time, with Leif at the rudder. Suddenly he changed course, commanding that the sails be brought in tight.

"Why do we sail so close to the wind?" asked one of the men. "This surely is folly. We'll never get home if we sail like this."

"Look out to sea, over there," said Leif. "Tell me what you see."

The man looked and said, "There's nothing there." Others of the crew looked and also said they saw nothing.

"I think there's a ship over there, or maybe a skerry," said Leif. "Look more closely."

The crew looked and agreed that there must be a skerry, but none of them understood why Leif would care about a bit of rock out in the middle of the sea.

"It's not just a bit of rock," said Leif. "I think there are people there. And if there are people there, they will need our help."

"Pirates, like as not," said one of the men. "We'll sail up to them, and then they'll board us and we'll have to fight for our lives."

"Be that as it may," said Leif, "we still have the advantage of them. And it would be a shameful thing to sail past without seeing whether they are friendly and in need of help or not."

They sailed as close to the skerry as they could and then dropped their anchor. Then Leif and a few other men lowered the rowboat into the water and rowed over to the skerry, where they found a group of fourteen men and one woman together on the rock with a pile of the cargo and belongings they had managed to save before their ship sank.

"Thank the gods you've come!" said one man. "We thought we had met our doom for sure."

"Which of you is the captain?" said Leif.

"I am," said another.

"What is your name?" asked Leif.

"I am Thorir, and I come from Norway. What is your name?"

"My name is Leif."

"Not Eirik's son, Eirik the Red of Brattahild in Greenland?" said Thorir.

"The very same," said Leif. "Come aboard my ship and I'll take you to Greenland, where you are welcome to stay or to find another ship to take you home. We'll bring as much of your cargo and belongings as my ship can hold, but the rest will have to stay here."

Thorir and his wife, Gudrid, and the others readily agreed to Leif's offer. They boarded Leif's ship with a good portion of their belongings and cargo, then sailed back to Brattahild, where Leif and his crew unloaded their ship.

"Won't you spend the winter with me and my father?" said Leif to Thorir and Gudrid. "I'll also see to it that your friends have lodgings so that no one goes without shelter."

Leif was as good as his word. He found lodgings for the thirteen men who he had rescued along with Thorir and Gudrid, and he also made sure his crew had places to go for the winter. When everyone saw what a wealth of timber and grapes Leif had brought back, and when they heard his tale of his sojourn in Vinland and the rescue of Thorir and his friends, they began calling Leif "the Lucky," since he had had so much good fortune on that journey.

The winter was not as gentle as the summer had been. Thorir and his crew all fell sick, and most of them died, including Thorir. The sickness did not spare Leif's family either, for his father, Eirik, also fell ill and died at that time.

Of Thorvald Eiriksson

Leif's adventure in Vinland was the talk of Greenland. Leif's brother, Thorvald, listened carefully to the stories and thought long about them. Finally he decided that he would try his own luck in the new land. He bought a ship and raised a crew of thirty after hearing all Leif had to tell about how to get to Vinland and where he had set up the houses. When the ship was provisioned and the crew ready, Thorvald set sail to Vinland and arrived at Leif's camp after an uneventful voyage.

They beached their ship and brought their provisions ashore. They made the houses ready and explored a little bit of the land around the camp. At the end of the day, Thorvald told his crew, "We will spend the winter here, and in the spring we will see what else this land has to offer."

The crew agreed that this was a good plan. They settled in for the winter and lived on the salmon that teemed in the river and the lake.

In the spring, Thorvald and his crew worked to repair the ship. When summer came, Thorvald sent a party of men in the ship's boat to explore the land to the west of them. The men explored along the coast throughout the summer, and when they returned that autumn, they had much to tell Thorvald and the others.

"The land is very fair," said the leader of the expedition. "There are thick forests and beaches of fine white sand. To the north, there are many small islands, and the sea in that place is quite shallow. We saw no other people, and no animals to speak of, the entire time we were on our journey.

"After we had explored the coast for a while, we rowed over to the islands. We found much the same there as we had on the headland, although we did find one thing made of wood that looked like what we use to cover stores of grain. That certainly was made by human hands, but we did not find the people who made it or any other signs of them."

The following summer, Thorvald and his crew decided to sail in the ship to the east to see what they might find there, leaving part of their number behind to keep watch over the houses. But Thorvald's new journey was not as fortunate as the one his men had made with the small boat the summer before. A storm blew up as Thorvald's ship rounded one headland. The wind and the waves drove the ship onto the rocks, cracking the keel. The men managed to get the ship safely onto the beach, and no lives were lost, but there was to be no more exploring for a long time because the ship had taken such heavy damage.

The men worked for many days putting in a new keel and repairing the sides of the ship. When they were finished, Thorvald said, "Let's set that broken keel up in a place of honor here. We'll call this place Kjalarnes [Keel Point]."

As soon as the ship was completely seaworthy, Thorvald and his men resumed their journey eastward along the coast. There they found some fjords and a cape that extended northward toward the sea. They beached their ship at the mouth of one of the fjords, and all went ashore. When they had walked some way inland, Thorvald looked about him and was very pleased by what he saw. "I think I shall settle here," he said. "This is a very fair place, indeed."

They returned to the ship, but one of Thorvald's companions looked along the beach and said, "Wait. Look there. What do you see?"

"I see three humps on the sand," said another of the men.

"Those weren't there before," said the first. "And I don't think they are part of the landscape."

"We'll divide into three groups," said Thorvald. "We'll go silently up to those humps, whatever they are, and deal with what we find there. Each group takes one hump. Ready? Let's go."

As Thorvald and his men crept closer, they saw that the humps were three small boats with skin coverings. They flipped the boats over, and under each one they found three men hiding. One man managed to escape in his boat, but Thorvald and his crew killed all the others.

Thorvald and his men then looked about them and saw what looked like hills farther down the fjord. "I don't think those are hills," said Thorvald. "I think those must be dwellings of some kind. Those nine men didn't just appear out of thin air."

The day had been a long and strenuous one. Thorvald and his men were exhausted. They lay down to rest right where they were, and soon all of them had fallen into a deep sleep. They did not awaken until they heard the sound of a voice calling to them. "Wake up!" cried the voice. "Wake up, Thorvald! Wake up all you sailors! Board your ship now if you value your lives! Wake up!"

The men all sprang up and looked down the fjord. Hundreds of skin boats like the ones they had found were now being paddled toward them, and every boat was full of fierce-looking warriors.

"Back to the ship!" cried Thorvald. "Back to the ship, and set the war shields on the gunwales as soon as may be. We will defend ourselves as well as we can, but try not to fight back if it isn't needed."

The men set the shields on the gunwales as the warriors in the boats rowed ever closer. The warriors had bows with them, and soon a hail of arrows was flying toward Thorvald and his companions, who sheltered behind the shields. After a time, the attacking warriors stopped shooting, then turned their boats around and paddled away.

"Is anyone hurt?" asked Thorvald.

All the men replied that they had taken no injuries.

"I was not so fortunate," said Thorvald. "One of those arrows managed to fly between two of the shields. It pierced my armpit." Thorvald showed the arrow to his friends. "I fear this wound will be the death of me. Take me back to the place that I thought so fair, and bury me there, with a cross at my head and a cross at my feet. Call that place Krossanes [Cross Point] when I am laid to rest as I asked." Thorvald then died, and his friends buried him with the crosses at his head and feet as he had asked, because Thorvald was a Christian.

When Thorvald had been properly laid to rest, the men took ship and sailed back to the houses. They had much to tell their companions who had stayed behind, and their companions had much to tell them. They decided to spend the winter there at the houses and sail back to Greenland in the spring, having laid in a cargo of grapes and grapevines.

Spring came, and the men sailed safely back to Greenland with a heavily laden ship. They steered their boat into the port at Eiriksfjord and were welcomed home with much joy by their friends and families. They met with Leif and told him all that had happened on their journey, and their tale was not a short one.

Of Thorstein Eiriksson

Eirik the Red had a third son who was named Thorstein. Thorstein married Gudrid, the widow of Thorir, who had been rescued along with her late husband and their ship's crew by Thorstein's brother, Leif. Thorstein wanted to go to Vinland to fetch the body of his brother, so that he might be laid in his own native soil rather than rest in a foreign land. Thorstein gathered a crew of twenty-five large, strong men, and put to sea with them and with his wife, Gudrid.

Thorstein's adventure went ill from the very beginning. Thorstein and his crew sailed to and fro on the open ocean, not able to find their way until winter was already settling in. "We can't find our way, and soon it will be too cold to sail," said Thorstein. "We'll return to Greenland and wait out the winter, and then try again when the warmer weather comes."

And so they sailed to Greenland, and they put in at Lysefjord, a settlement in the west. When they arrived, Thorstein arranged winter lodgings for all his crew, but was unable to find a place for himself and his wife, for Christianity had only lately come to Greenland. They camped on the beach next to their ship for two nights. On the day after the second night, some men came to Thorstein's tent. "Who is there inside the tent?" they asked.

"There are two of us here," said Thorstein. "Who is asking?"

One of the men said, "My name is also Thorstein, but I am also known as Thorstein the Black. I have come to ask you to spend the winter with me in my home."

"That is a generous offer," said Thorstein Eiriksson, "but first I must ask my wife whether she agrees."

Thorstein Eiriksson asked Gudrid what she thought of the offer.

"If you think it acceptable," she said, "then we should accept."

Thorstein Eiriksson said to the men outside the tent, "My wife agrees, and we gladly accept your offer of hospitality."

"That is good," said Thorstein the Black. "I will come back tomorrow to fetch you and your belongings. I can't promise that it will be a merry winter, for both my wife Grimhild and I are very staid and set in our ways, and I prefer my own company. We also have a different religion from you, but it seems to me that yours is better than mine."

The next day, Thorstein the Black came to the beach as promised. He helped Thorstein Eiriksson and Gudrid load their belongings onto his cart, and then drove them and their things back to his home. Thorstein the Black and his wife were very generous to their guests, and provided well for them throughout the winter.

Gudrid acquitted herself well in the house of her hosts. She was a very beautiful woman, and also a wise one who knew how to behave with strangers.

The winter had barely begun in earnest when an illness struck Lysefjord. Many of Thorstein Eiriksson's crew fell ill, and some of them died.

"Do not lay the bodies of my crew to rest here," said Thorstein Eiriksson. "I wish to take them back home to Eiriksfjord for burial when the summer comes."

The home of Thorstein the Black was not spared from the plague either. Grimhild fell ill, even though she was a large woman and just as strong as a man. Thorstein Eiriksson fell ill soon after Grimhild, and Grimhild died soon after that.

When Grimhild was dead, her husband said, "I am going out to find a plank to lay her body upon."

"Don't be too long, dear Thorstein," said Gudrid.

"I shan't tarry," said Thorstein, and then he left the room.

After Thorstein the Black had gone, Thorstein Eiriksson said, "Why is Grimhild behaving that way? She is pushing herself up on her elbow. She is trying to get out of bed and trying to find her shoes."

Just then, Thorstein the Black returned with a plank to lay his wife's body on, and the body of Grimhild fell back onto the bed with such force that every beam in the house creaked.

Thorstein the Black made a good coffin for his wife and laid her gently in it. When the coffin had been sealed, Thorstein the Black took it out of the house for burial. This took all the effort he could muster, even though he was a very strong man, for Grimhild was a very large and very strong woman.

The sorrows of that household were not yet over, for soon Thorstein Eiriksson also died. Gudrid and Thorstein the Black were there at his bedside when he gave up the ghost, and Gudrid was sorely grieved that her husband was no more.

Thorstein the Black was moved to pity by Gudrid's weeping. He picked her up and held her on his lap as he would a small child, and spoke words of comfort and encouragement to her. He also promised that Thorstein Eiriksson's body would be taken back to Eiriksfjord with the bodies of his crew, so that they all could be laid to rest together in the place that was their home. Thorstein the Black also told Gudrid that he would find other people to join them in his house so that she might be less lonely.

"Thank you, dear friend," said Gudrid. "I am grateful for your help and comfort."

Just then, the body of Thorstein Eiriksson sat up in the bed. "Where is Gudrid?" it asked.

Gudrid did not answer, and neither did Thorstein the Black.

The body of Thorstein Eiriksson asked twice more, "Where is Gudrid?"

Gudrid said to Thorstein the Black, "Should I answer it?"

"No, do not answer," he replied. "I will speak for you."

Then Thorstein the Black went over to the bed and knelt beside it. "Tell me what you want, dearest friend and bearer of my name. I am here."

For a moment, there was silence. Then the corpse spoke. "I have a message for Gudrid. I know what her fate is, and I want to tell her of myself so that she might not mourn so heavily. I have gone to a very good place where I shall rest well. Hear me, Gudrid, for what I say is true: You will marry an Icelander, and together you will have a long life and many children, all of them good and strong and sweet. You and your husband will leave Greenland and go to Norway for a time, and after that you will settle in Iceland, which will become your home. After your husband dies, you will make a pilgrimage to Rome. When you return to Iceland, a church will be built on your farm there, and you will take the holy vows of a nun. There you will stay until your death."

Then the body of Thorstein Eiriksson fell back on the bed. His body was prepared for burial and taken to his ship.

Thorstein the Black kept all the promises he had made to Gudrid. When the spring came, he sold his farm and his livestock. Then he took Gudrid and all her belongings to the ship where her husband's body lay, then sailed back to Eiriksfjord, where he saw to it that Thorstein Eiriksson and all his companions were laid to rest in the Christian churchyard as was right and proper for men of their faith.

Gudrid went to live with her brother-in-law Leif at Brattahild, while Thorstein the Black made his home in Eiriksfjord. Thorstein lived there for the rest of his days, and he was well respected by everyone for his generous spirit.

Of Thorfinn Karlsefni

The summer that Thorstein Eiriksson was laid to rest in Eiriksfjord, a very wealthy man named Thorfinn Karlsefni came to Iceland from Norway. Thorfinn lodged with Leif Eiriksson the following winter, and soon he fell in love with Gudrid, the widow of Thorstein Eiriksson. One day, Thorfinn went to Gudrid and said, "I find that I love you very much, and would be honored if you would be my wife."

"I cannot answer now," said Gudrid, "but I will let you know soon."

Gudrid then went to her brother-in-law and told him of Thorfinn's proposal. "I would rather you answered Thorfinn on my behalf," said Gudrid.

"Do you approve of Thorfinn?" asked Leif. "Are you willing to marry him?"

"I am," said Gudrid. "He seems to be a good man."

Then Leif went to Thorfinn and told him that Gudrid accepted his proposal. They were wed later that same winter.

Now, Leif had been home from his voyage to Vinland for some time, but everyone still spoke of his adventures, and of the adventures of Thorvald and his crew. Many people urged Thorfinn to try his luck in Vinland. Thorfinn's wife, Gudrid, was among those.

Finally Thorfinn agreed. He hired a crew of sixty men and five women. They agreed to split the profits from the voyage equally among them. They also gathered livestock to take with them since they wanted to settle permanently in Vinland if possible.

Thorfinn went to Leif and said, "As you know, I am planning a voyage to Vinland. May I have the houses you built there?"

"I will gladly lend them to you," said Leif, "but I will not give them to you to be your own."

Thorfinn agreed to these terms and set sail as soon as he had a fair wind. It did not take long for his ships to arrive in Vinland. Everyone went ashore and set their bedding inside the houses. They then set their livestock free to look for pasturage and went looking for food for themselves. It did not take long for them to find good things to eat, for a rorqual had beached itself not far from the houses. The rorqual was still fresh, so Thorfinn and his crew butchered it. They ate very well that night and for many days afterward, and the animals found good grazing a little way inland from the houses. Soon the male animals became very restless and difficult to handle, not least the bull they had brought with them.

Once they had settled in, Thorfinn said, "Let us fell much timber now and leave it out to dry. We can take it back with us next summer and make a good profit from it."

This was done, and soon they had a good load of timber laid out on some stones. They also worked at gathering grapes, fishing in the river, and hunting game, both for their food at that time and to store away for the winter that was fast approaching.

When the warm weather came after their first winter at the houses, they had their first encounter with the people who were native to that land. A group of men carrying bundles of furs came out of the forest very close to the cattle pasture. The arrival of the strangers angered the bull, who snorted and pawed the ground at them. The native men had never seen a bull before. They were very frightened and ran to Thorfinn's house to get away from the angry animal.

The native men begged to be allowed into the house, but Thorfinn would not let them enter. For some time, Thorfinn and the native men shouted at one another, but since they did not understand each other's language, this was of no avail. Finally the men set their bundles of furs down on the ground in front of the houses and waited for Thorfinn and the others to come out to them.

When Thorfinn and his crew saw that the men had come to trade, they went out to greet them and see what they might exchange for the furs. The native men were greatly interested in the weapons and tools that Thorfinn and his crew had brought with them, but Thorfinn forbade trading anything made of metal. The Icelanders decided to see whether the native men would accept a gift of milk from the cows in exchange for the furs. The native people were greatly pleased with the milk. They drank all that Thorfinn's company gave them, then headed back to their own homes, leaving their furs and skins behind in exchange for the milk.

Once the native people had gone, Thorfinn said, "We need to be prepared to defend ourselves. Let us cut timber and build a palisade around our farm in case the native people become hostile."

Not long after the visit of the native men, Gudrid gave birth to a fine son. Thorfinn and Gudrid named him Snorri.

Early the next winter, the native men returned to Thorfinn's settlement, bearing bundles of furs and skins. When Thorfinn saw this, he said, "Milk the cows, and bring the milk out to the men in exchange for the furs. Do not give them anything else."

When the native men saw the cows being milked, they tossed their bundles over the palisade wall.

Now, while this was going on, Gudrid was sitting just inside the doorway of one of the houses, tending her little son, Snorri. While she rocked Snorri in his cradle, a shadow fell across the doorway. Gudrid looked up, and there she saw a strange woman. The woman was very short and had enormous eyes. She wore a tunic that closely fitted her body and a scarf over her hair. The strange woman came inside the doorway and asked, "What is your name?"

Gudrid replied, "My name is Gudrid. What is your name?"

"I am also Gudrid," said the strange woman.

Just as Thorfinn's wife was about to offer the stranger a place to sit, there was a loud crash as of thunder, and the strange woman disappeared. At the same time this happened, one of Thorfinn's men killed one of the natives for trying to steal weapons. The other natives then ran away, leaving all their goods behind. When Gudrid asked the others whether they had seen the strange woman, everyone said they had not.

Later that day, Thorfinn gathered all his crew together. He said to them, "I doubt the native people will leave us in peace much longer. We killed one of their own, and it's likely that they will be hostile when they come back. We need to have a plan for what to do when that happens. This is what we will do: Ten men will go to that headland over there and let themselves be seen by the natives. The rest of us will take our cattle into the forest, where we will cut a clearing for them. When they come at us through the forest, we will loose the bull on them before attacking them ourselves."

The others agreed to this plan. They chose a place with the lake on one side and the forest on the other to make the clearing.

It did not take long before a large group of native men came to where Thorfinn and the others waited with the cattle. There was a fight, and many of the native men were killed. One of the native men was very tall and good-looking; Thorfinn thought that this must be the chief of that people. Another of the native men found an axe that had been dropped during the fight. He looked at it for a moment, then swung it at one of his companions, killing him on the spot. The tall, handsome man grabbed the axe away from the one who had found it, and threw it as far as he could into the lake. Then all the native men ran away from that place, and troubled Thorfinn and his companions no more.

Thorfinn and the others spent another winter there, but when spring came, Thorfinn said, "I won't stay here any longer. I think we should all go back to Greenland. Let's load our ships with the timber and other good things that we can sell at home, and call an end to this adventure."

The others agreed that this was the best plan. They loaded their ships with the timber they had cut and with many grapevines and fine pelts. They set sail as soon as everything was ready, and after an uneventful voyage, they arrived safely at Eiriksfjord, where they spent the winter.

The following summer, Thorfinn readied his ship to sail to Norway. He had fair winds and arrived there after a brief voyage. He and his wife stayed in Norway for the winter, and they made a fair profit on the goods they had brought back from Vinland. The nobles of that place were very impressed with Thorfinn and Gudrid, and treated the two very well the whole time they were there.

In the spring, Thorfinn and Gudrid sailed for Iceland. They landed at Skagafjord, and when the ship had been brought ashore and secured against the winter weather, they went to Glaumbaer, where they bought land, built a house, and began to farm. Everyone in Glaumbaer and the surrounding lands were pleased that Thorfinn had come to settle among them, for he was thought to be a very fine man of good reputation. He and his wife had many children. They were a happy family and beloved of all their neighbors.

When Thorfinn died, Gudrid ran the farm herself. Snorri, her son who had been born in Vinland, helped her in this. Snorri found himself a good woman to be his wife, and they were soon wed. After the wedding, Gudrid went to Snorri and said, "You are a man full grown, with a beautiful wife who is a good woman. I give you this farm to be your own, for I am now going to go on a pilgrimage. I hope to go all the way to Rome. I wish all good blessings on you, on your wife, and on your children who are yet to come."

After Gudrid had left on her pilgrimage, Snorri had a church built there in Glaumbaer, and when Gudrid returned, she took vows as a nun and lived a monastic life at the church.

Thorfinn and Gudrid's children did very well for themselves, and were blessed, as Gudrid had said they would be. Snorri's son Thorgeir had a daughter named Yngveld, and her son Brand became a bishop. Snorri's daughter Hallfrid married a man named Runolf, and their son Thorlak also became a bishop. Snorri's brother, Bjorn, had a daughter named Thorunn, and her son, named Bjorn like his father, also became a bishop.

Thorfinn Karlsefni's family was very large and very prosperous. Everyone respected them, and they had a large number of descendants. It was Thorfinn who told most of the stories about these voyages, the tales of which have now been set down in writing.

Of Freydis Eiriksdottir

On the day that Thorfinn, Gudrid, and their crew returned from Vinland, their ships sitting low in the water beneath loads of timber and other good things, the people of Eiriksfjord once again began talking of voyaging west to seek their own fortunes.

During that summer, two men from Norway arrived in Greenland. Their names were Helgi and Finnbogi, and they were brothers. They had been born in Iceland, in the Eastfjords. They found lodging and spent the winter in Greenland.

Now, Eirik the Red had a daughter named Freydis, and she lived at Gardar with her husband, Thorvard. She had heard of the two men from Norway and had been harboring thoughts of her own about a voyage to Greenland. Freydis went to the place where Helgi and Finnbogi were staying, and asked them whether they would like to be partners with her in a voyage to Vinland.

"We'll take your ship and mine," she said, "and whatever profits we make we will split equally among us."

"This is acceptable," said the brothers, and so the three of them began planning their voyage together.

Freydis went to her brother, Leif, and said, "Give me the houses that you have built in Vinland."

Leif replied, "I'll not give them to you, but you may borrow them for as long as you need them."

Freydis agreed with Helgi and Finnbogi that they would each take thirty men and some women with them aboard their ships. Freydis broke her word almost immediately by taking five extra men, concealing them aboard her ship until they arrived in Vinland, when it was too late to do anything about it.

Now, they agreed to sail together in convoy, and so the ships were never very far apart from one another, but Helgi's and Finnbogi's ship managed to arrive some time before Freydis's. When she disembarked, she found that Helgi and Finnbogi and their crews had begun putting away their belongings in some of the houses.

When Freydis arrived with her crew and their belongings, she saw what Helgi and Finnbogi had done. "Why have you moved into these houses with all your belongings?" she asked.

"We had an agreement," said Helgi. "We get to stay in the houses too, as we discussed before we left."

"No, we didn't agree to that, and neither did my brother," said Freydis. "Leif lent these houses to me, not to you. Pack up your things and get out. Build your own houses somewhere else."

"This is a wicked thing you do, Freydis," said Helgi. "Finnbogi and I would never stoop to such things."

And so Helgi, Finnbogi, and their crews went inland a little way and built a large house on the shore of the lake. While the brothers were building their house, Freydis ordered her crew to begin felling trees to make a cargo of timber.

When winter came, the brothers went to Freydis and said, "We should visit one another's houses during the winter. We can play games and make merry, just as we do at home at this time of the year."

Freydis agreed, but it did not take long before quarrels broke out between Freydis's people and the brothers' crews. The two groups stopped visiting one another, and so Helgi and Finnbogi's plan for a merry winter came to naught.

One morning, Freydis awoke very early while everyone else in the house was asleep. She got out of bed without waking her husband, got dressed, and put on her husband's cloak, but she did not put on any shoes. The grass was heavy with dew at that time. Freydis walked through the wet grass to the brothers' house. There she found the door ajar. She pushed it open and waited in the doorway. Finnbogi saw her standing there. From his bed at the other end of the house, he said, "What do you want, Freydis?"

"Come outside and talk to me," she said.

Finnbogi agreed. They went over to the trunk of a fallen tree and sat down for their talk.

"Are things well with you?" asked Freydis.

"Yes," said Finnbogi. "This country is a very agreeable place, and I'm glad I came. But it is a sorrowful thing that there is such ill feeling between us and between our crews."

"I agree," said Freydis, "but that is not why I have come to speak with you. I have come to ask that you exchange ships with me. Your ship is larger than mine, and I want to leave this place."

"Very well," said Finnbogi. "There's probably no point in denying you. I will trade you my ship for yours."

Then Finnbogi went back to his bed, and Freydis walked back to the houses, where everyone was still asleep. Freydis climbed into bed next to her husband, but because her feet were so wet and cold from her walk through the dew, it woke him up.

"Hey, there!" said Thorvard. "Why are your feet so cold and wet?"

"I went to visit Helgi and Finnbogi. I wanted to trade my ship for theirs. My request made them very angry, and they beat me and called me foul names. You likely won't do anything about it. Everyone knows you're a coward, and you probably won't stand up for me. It's too bad we're not in Greenland; my brothers would definitely do something about this insult. But since we're not in Greenland, all I can do is tell you that if you don't avenge me, I'll divorce you on the spot."

Thorvard was ashamed by what Freydis had said, and became angry. He woke the men of the house and told them to get their weapons and follow him. Thorvard, Freydis, and the others went to Helgi and Finnbogi's house, where Thorvard and his men took prisoner all the men who were inside. When they were all tied up outside the house, Thorvard said, "What do we do with them now?"

"Kill them," said Freydis.

"All of them?" asked Thorvard.

"Yes," said Freydis. "It's the only way."

And so it was that Freydis had all the men who came with Helgi and Finnbogi killed. Then she had the women brought out of the house.

"Give me that axe," said Freydis to one of her men. He gave it to her, and she killed each of the five women who had come with Helgi and Finnbogi.

Then Freydis, Thorvard, and their men went back to Leif's houses. When they arrived, Freydis said, "When we get back to Greenland, none of you are to breathe a word of what just happened. If you do, I will find you, and I will kill you. We will tell everyone that the others decided to settle here and that they gave us their ship to take our cargo home."

In the spring, Freydis and her crew loaded both ships with the goods they had collected during their sojourn in Vinland. They sailed with fair winds all the way back to Eiriksfjord, where Thorfinn Karlsefni was preparing to depart for Norway. Everyone looked at the cargo Freydis brought back with her, and all agreed that this was the greatest amount of goods anyone had yet brought home from Vinland, and by far the most valuable.

Freydis went back to her farm after rewarding her crew very generously so that they would not talk about what had happened in Vinland. Then Freydis resumed working her farm and taking care of her livestock.

Now, there were some among Freydis's crew who were unable to keep silent about what she had done. Soon enough, word spread that Freydis had had Helgi and Finnbogi's crew murdered and that she had killed all the women herself. Eventually, Freydis's brother Leif heard the story, and he was horrified. He had three of Freydis's crew arrested, and he tortured them until they told the whole story. When he had heard everything, Leif said, "I am not the one to punish my sister for her cruel deeds. But I think that her children and her children's children will not fare well. That shall be recompense enough."

Leif's words came true. When Freydis and Thorvard had children, everyone treated them badly because they expected them to behave as their mother had. And when those children had children of their own, people treated them badly as well for the same reason.

Thus ends the Vinland Sagas.

References

Boult, Katharine F. *Heroes of the Northlands: Their Stories Retold.* London: J. M. Dent & Co., 1903.

Chadwick, Nora. *Stories and Ballads of the Far Past.* Cambridge: Cambridge University Press, 1921.

Edwards, Paul, and Hermann Pálsson, ed. and trans. *Arrow-Odd: A Medieval Novel.* New York: New York University Press, 1970.

Gathorne-Hardy, Geoffrey Malcolm, trans. *The Norse Discoverers of America: The Wineland Sagas.* Oxford: Clarendon Press, 1921.

Jones, Gwyn. *The Norse Atlantic Saga.* New ed. Oxford: Oxford University Press, 1964.

Kolodny, Annette. *In Search of First Contact: The Vikings of Vinland, the People of Dawnland, and the Anglo-American Anxiety of Discovery.* Durham: Duke University Press, 2012.

Kunz, Keneva, trans. "The Vinland Sagas." In *The Sagas of Icelanders: A Selection*, pp. 626–76. New York: Viking Penguin, 2000.

Magnusson, Magnus, and Hermann Pálsson. *The Vinland Sagas: The Norse Discovery of America.* New York: New York University Press, 1966.

Munch, Peter Andreas. *Norse Mythology: Legends of Gods and Heroes*. Trans. Sigurd Bernhard Hustvedt. New York: The American-Scandinavian Foundation 1926.

Pringle, Heather. "Evidence of Viking Outpost found in Canada." *National Geographic News* (19 October 2012). <https://www.nationalgeographic.com/news/2012/10/121019-viking-outpost-second-new-canada-science-sutherland/#close> Accessed 25 May 2020.

Reeves, Arthur Middleton, North Ludlow Beamish, and Rasmus B. Anderson, trans. *Norroena: The History and Romance of Northern Europe*. Vol. 15, *Vinland Edition*. n. c.: n. p., T. H. Smart, 1906.

Simpson, Jaqueline, trans. *The Northmen Talk: A Choice of Tales from Iceland*. London: Phoenix House, 1965.

Tolkien, Christopher, trans. *Saga Heidriks Konungs ins Vitra/The Saga of King Heidrik the Wise*. London: Thomas Nelson and Sons, Ltd., 1960.

Tunstall, Peter, trans. *The Saga of Hervor & King Heidrik the Wise*. In *The Complete Fornaldarsögur Nederlanda: Legendary Sagas of the Northland in English Translation*. <http://www.germanicmythology.com/FORNALDARSAGAS/HervararSagaTunstall.html> Accessed 8 April 2020.

Waggoner, Ben, trans. *The Hrafnista Sagas*. New Haven: Troth Publications, 2012.

Wallace, Birgitta. "The Norse in Newfoundland: L'Anse aux Meadows and Vinland." *Newfoundland and Labrador Studies* 19/1. Retrieved from https://journals.lib.unb.ca/index.php/NFLDS/article/view/140.

n. a. *Norse Tales of Legends, Gods & Heroes*. Stamford: Longmeadow Press, 1996.

Boult, Katherine F. *Asgard & the Norse Heroes*. London: J. M. Dent & Sons, Ltd., [1914].

Bartlett, R. "The Viking Hiatus in the Cult of Saints as Seen in the Twelfth Century." In *The Long Twelfth-Century View of the Anglo-Saxon Past*, edited by Martin Brett and David A. Woodman, 13-25. Abingdon: Routledge, 2016.

Burns, Marjorie J. *Perilous Realms: Celtic and Norse in Tolkien's Middle-earth.* Toronto: University of Toronto Press, 2005.

Carpenter, Humphrey. *Tolkien: A Biography.* Boston: Houghton Mifflin Company, 1977.

Crawford, Jackson, trans. *The Saga of the Volsungs, with the Saga of Ragnar Lothbrok.* Indianapolis: Hackett Publishing Company, Inc., 2017.

Edminson, John P. *Stories from the Norseland.* Philadelphia: The Penn Publishing Co., 1909.

Elton, Oliver, trans. *The Nine Books of the Danish History of Saxo Grammaticus.* 2 vols. London: Norroena Society, [1905].

Evans, Jonathan. "The Dragon-Lore of Middle Earth: Tolkien and Old English and Old Norse Tradition." In *J. R. R. Tolkien and His Literary Resonances: Views of Middle Earth*, edited by George Clark and Daniel Timmons, 21-38. Westport: Greenwood Press, 2000.

Graham-Campbell, James, ed. *Cultural Atlas of the Viking World.* Oxford: Andromeda, 1994.

Guerber, Helene Adeline. *Legends of the Middle Ages.* New York: American Book Company, 1929.

Hall, Richard. *The World of the Vikings.* New York: Thames and Hudson, 2007.

Haywood, John. Northmen: *The Viking Saga A.D. 793-1241.* New York: Thomas Dunne Books, 2015.

Heaney, Seamus, trans. *Beowulf.* New York: Farrar, Straus & Gerous, 2000.

Hendenstierna-Jonson, Charlotte, et al. "A Female Viking Warrior Confirmed by Genomics." *American Journal of Physical Anthropology* 164/4 (2017): 853-60.

Jesch, Judith. *Women in the Viking Age*. Woodbridge: The Boydell Press, 1991.

Kidder, Daniel P. *Stories of the Norsemen*. Rev. ed. New York: Carlton & Phillips, 1854.

Magnusson, Eirikr, and William M. Morris. *The Volsunga Saga*. London: Norroena Society, 1906.

Mawer, Allen. "Ragnar Lothbrok and His Sons." *The Saga Book of the Viking Club* 6 (1909): 68-89.

Morris, Charles. *Historical Tales: The Romance of Reality*. Vol. 9, *Scandinavian*. Philadelphia: J. B. Lippincott and Company, 1908.

Munch, Peter. *Norse Mythology: Legends of Gods and Heroes*. Trans. Sigurd Bernhard Hustvedt. New York: American-Scandinavian Foundation, 1926.

Oliver, Neil. *The Vikings: A New History*. New York: Pegasus Books LLC, 2013.

Resnick, Henry. "The Hobbit-Forming World of J. R. R. Tolkien." *The Saturday Evening Post* (2 July 1966): 90-94.

Schlauch, Margaret, trans. *The Saga of the Volsungs: The Saga of Ragnar Lodbrok Together with the Lay of Kraka*. New York: The American Scandinavian Foundation, 1930.

Speight, E. E. *Children of Odin*. Rev. ed. London: Horace Marshall & Son, [1903].

St. Clair, Gloriana. "An Overview of the Northern Influences on Tolkien's Works." *Mythlore: A Journal of J. R. R. Tolkien, C. S. Lewis, Charles Williams, and Mythopoeic Literature* 2 (1996): 63-67.

Taggart, Caroline. *The Book of English Place Names: How Our Towns and Villages Got Their Names*. n. p.: Ebury Press, 2011.

Tolkien, J. R. R. *The Silmarillion.* Ed. Christopher Tolkien. Boston: Houghton Mifflin Company, 1977.

——. *Smith of Wootton Major and Farmer Giles of Ham.* n.c.: Ballantine Books, 1972.

——. *The Hobbit.* Boston: Houghton Mifflin Company, 1966.

——. "On Fairy-Stories." In *Essays Presented to Charles Williams,* pp. 38-89. London: Oxford University Press, 1947.

Waggoner, Ben, trans. *The Sagas of Ragnar Lodbrok.* New Haven: The Troth, 2009.

Welles, Albert. *The Pedigree and History of the Washington Family.* New York: Society Library, 1879.

Wheaton, Henry. *History of the Northmen, or Danes and Normans, from the Earliest Times to the Conquest of England.* London: J. Murray, 1831.

Winroth, Anders. *The Age of the Vikings.* Princeton: Princeton University Press, 2014.

Wolf, Kirsten. *Daily Life of the Vikings.* Westport: The Greenwood Press, 2004.

Here's another book by Matt Clayton that you might be interested in

[i] Kirsten Wolf, *Daily Life of the Vikings* (Westport: The Greenwood Press, 2004), p. 22.
[ii] Wolf, *Daily Life*, p. 22.
[iii] Wolf, *Daily Life*, p. 22.
[iv] Richard Hall, *The World of the Vikings* (New York: Thames and Hudson, 2007), pp. 40-43.
[v] Anders Winroth, *The Age of the Vikings* (Princeton: Princeton University Press, 2014), pp. 138-9.
[vi] James Graham-Campbell, ed., *Cultural Atlas of the Viking World* (Oxford: Andromeda, 1994), p. 63.
[vii] Graham-Campbell, *Cultural Atlas*, pp. 80-83.
[viii] Wolf, *Daily Life*, p. 8.
[ix] Wolf, *Daily Life*, pp. 10-11.
[x] Wolf, *Daily Life*, pp. 22-24.
[xi] Winroth, *Age of the Vikings*, pp. 164-65.
[xii] The stories of women warriors in Saxo's history are summarized in Judith Jesch, *Women in the Viking Age* (Woodbridge: The Boydell Press, 1991), pp. 176ff.
[xiii] Charlotte Hendenstierna-Jonson et al., "A Female Viking Warrior Confirmed by Genomics," *American Journal of Physical Anthropology* 164/4 (2017): 853-60.
[xiv] Hendenstierna-Jonson et al., "Female Viking Warrior," p. 855.
[xv] Hendenstierna-Jonson et al., "Female Viking Warrior," p. 855-57.
[xvi] Hall, *World of the Vikings*, p. 34.
[xvii] Jesch, *Women in the Viking Age*, pp. 183-85.
[xviii] Wolf, *Daily Life*, p. 13.
[xix] Wolf, *Daily Life*, pp. 8-9.
[xx] Wolf, *Daily Life*, p. 10.
[xxi] Wolf, *Daily Life*, p. 10.
[xxii] Winroth, *Age of the Vikings*, pp. 162-64.
[xxiii] Winroth, *Age of the Vikings*, pp. 162-64.
[xxiv] Winroth, *Age of the Vikings*, pp. 163-64.
[xxv] Neil Oliver, *The Vikings: A New History* (New York: Pegasus Books LLC, 2013), p. 108.
[xxvi] Winroth, *Age of the Vikings*, p. 123.
[xxvii] John Haywood, *Northmen: The Viking Saga AD 793-1241* (New York: St. Martin's Press, 2015), p. 14.
[xxviii] Wolf, *Daily Life*, p. 24; Graham-Campbell, *Cultural Atlas*, p. 75.
[xxix] Haywood, *Northmen*, pp. 20-22; Graham-Campell, *Cultural Atlas*, p. 75.
[xxx] Haywood, *Northmen*, p. 22.
[xxxi] Graham-Campbell, *Cultural Atlas*, p. 75.
[xxxii] Graham-Campbell, *Cultural Atlas*, p. 79.

[xxxiii] Wolf, *Daily Life*, p. 24.
[xxxiv] Graham-Campbell, *Cultural Atlas*, p. 78.
[xxxv] Graham-Campbell, *Cultural Atlas*, p. 78.
[xxxvi] Hall, *World of the Vikings*, pp. 33, 99.
[xxxvii] Hall, *World of the Vikings*, p. 101.
[xxxviii] Hall, *World of the Vikings*, p. 101.
[xxxix] Winroth, *Age of the Vikings*, pp. 124-27,
[xl] Graham-Campbell, *Cultural Atlas*, p. 78.
[xli] Graham-Campbell, *Cultural Atlas*, p. 85.
[xlii] Hall, *World of the Vikings*, p. 59.
[xliii] Hall, *World of the Vikings*, p. 60.
[xliv] Hall, *World of the Vikings*, p. 60. Ribe is a town in Denmark.
[xlv] Haywood, *Northmen*, pp. 42-3.
[xlvi] Haywood, *Northmen*, p. 45.
[xlvii] Haywood, *Northmen*, pp. 45, 88.
[xlviii] Haywood, *Northmen*, pp. 169-70.
[xlix] Haywood, *Northmen*, p. 40.
[l] Winroth, *Age of the Vikings*, p. 136.
[li] Winroth, *Age of the Vikings*, pp. 136-39.
[lii] Winroth, *Age of the Vikings*, pp. 136-37.
[liii] Oliver, *New History*, pp. 99-100.
[liv] Hall, *Vikings*, p. 54.
[lv] Winroth, *Age of the Vikings*, p. 75.
[lvi] Haywood, *Northmen*, p. 47.
[lvii] Haywood, *Northmen*, p. 50.
[lviii] Oliver, New History, p. 169.
[lix] Caroline Taggart, *The Book of English Place Names: How Our Towns and Villages Got Their Names* (n. p.: Ebury Press, 2011), pp. 15, 82, 269.
[lx] Graham-Campbell, *Cultural Atlas*, pp. 190-91; Winroth, *Age of the Vikings*, p. 114.
[lxi] Graham-Campbell, *Cultural Atlas*, pp. 190-91.
[lxii] Graham-Campbell, *Cultural Atlas*, p. 192; Hall, *Vikings*, p. 97.
[lxiii] Hall, *Vikings*, pp. 150, 152.
[lxiv] Hall, *Vikings*, p. 151.
[lxv] Hall, *Vikings*, p. 181.
[lxvi] Hall, *Vikings*, p. 160.
[lxvii] Hall, *Vikings*, p. 161.
[lxviii] Ben Waggoner, trans., *The Sagas of Ragnar Lodbrok* (New Haven: The Troth, 2009), p. xiii.
[lxix] Waggoner, *Sagas of Ragnar Lodbrok*, p. xi.
[lxx] Waggoner, *Sagas of Ragnar Lodbrok*, p. xiii.
[lxxi] Waggoner, *Sagas of Ragnar Lodbrok*, p. xxiv. The manuscript in question is Copenhagen, Royal Danish Library, MS NkS 1824b 4to.

[lxxii] This manuscript is Copenhagen, Royal Danish Library, MS AM 147 4to. Waggoner, *Sagas of Ragnar Lodbrok*, p. xxiv.
[lxxiii] Waggoner, *Sagas of Ragnar Lodbrok*, p. xxv. Waggoner also notes that the *Hauksbók* was broken up into its constituent pieces, and the pieces were rebound and catalogued separately. The portion containing the *Tale of Ragnar's Sons* now resides in the Arnamagnaean Institute at the University of Copenhagan as MS AM 544.
[lxxiv] Robert Crawford, *Scotland's Books: A History of Scottish Literature* (Oxford: Oxford University Press, 2009), n. p., accessed through Google Books <http://google.com/books> 23 March 2020.
[lxxv] n. a., "Teutonic Forms," p. 3 (PDF accessed via https://www.jsicmail.ac.uk, 23 March 2020). The PDF appears to cite Turville-Petre, p. xix, as a source for the definition of *háttlausa* but does not give a bibliographical description beyond the author's surname and page number. It is possible that this information was taken from *Scaldic Poetry* by Gabriel Turville-Petre (Oxford: Clarendon Press, 1976), p. xxix, but I do not have access to this volume and so cannot confirm the accuracy of this assumption.
[lxxvi] Waggoner, *Sagas of Ragnar Lodbrok*, p. x.
[lxxvii] Oliver Elton, trans. *The Nine Books of the Danish History of Saxo Grammaticus.* 2 vols. (London: Norroena Society, [1905]).
[lxxviii] Elton, trans., *Saxo Grammaticus*, vol. 2, pp. 544-5.
[lxxix] Elton, trans., *Saxo Grammaticus*, vol. 2, pp. 550 (Charlemagne episode) and 552-4 (Hellespont episode).
[lxxx] Winroth, *Age of the Vikings*, pp. 134-38.
[lxxxi] Wolf, *Daily Life*, p. 55.
[lxxxii] Wolf, *Daily Life*, p. 55.
[lxxxiii] Crawford, *Volsungs*, p. xv.
[lxxxiv] R. Bartlett, "The Viking Hiatus in the Cult of Saints as Seen in the Twelfth Century," in *The Long Twelfth-Century View of the Anglo-Saxon Past*, edited by Martin Brett and David A. Woodman (Abingdon: Routledge, 2016), p. 18. Bartlett cites the F manuscript of the *Chronicle*, f. 54. "Viking Hiatus," n. 16.
[lxxxv] Bartlett, "Viking Hiatus," pp. 17-8.
[lxxxvi] Bartlett, "Viking Hiatus," p. 18.
[lxxxvii] Waggoner, *Sagas of Ragnar Lodbrok*, pp. xvi-xvii.
[lxxxviii] Crawford, *Volsungs*, p. xix.
[lxxxix] Albert Welles, *The Pedigree and History of the Washington Family* (New York: Society Library, 1879).
[xc] Welles, *Washington*, p. iv.
[xci] In one medieval version of the saga, Ragnar states that he is fifteen years old in his verse to Thora, but this version does not include Ragnar's sojourn with Lagertha. Because I am including the story about Ragnar meeting and marrying Lagertha prior to his encounter with the dragon, I have changed

Ragnar's age to eighteen to take his three years with Lagertha into account.

[xcii] A kenning for "dragon."

[xciii] Another kenning for "dragon."

[xciv] A kenning for "black." This is also a play on the name "Kraka," which itself means "crow."

[xcv] The original sources are unclear about what the exact nature of Ivar's disability was. In some ways, the descriptions seem to suggest a milder form of brittle bone disease (*osteogenesis imperfecta*), but they could also refer to rickets. Rickets is a childhood ailment that leads to a softening of the bones, which is caused by a lack of vitamin D. Effects of this softening include bow-leggedness and knock knees, which impairs one's ability to walk. Rickets is more common in northern latitudes because of the lack of sunlight during a significant part of the year. It can also be caused by genetic factors or by the mother having a severe vitamin D deficiency during pregnancy.

[xcvi] Kraka/Aslaug's father also had the ability to understand the speech of birds, which he acquired by accidentally tasting some of the dragon Fafnir's blood while roasting its heart for Regin, the blacksmith to whom Sigurd was apprenticed and who was the brother of Fafnir.

[xcvii] "Fafnirsbane" means "Killer of Fafnir."

[xcviii] Although the saga was only written down in Christian times, one wonders whether the pit of snakes was intended to be some kind of reference to the pagan concept either of Hvergelmir or of Nastrandir. The latter was a place in the Norse underworld that was made out of venomous serpents, and the former was a place inhabited by a giant serpent. Nastrandir was the place to which the souls of oathbreakers and murderers were consigned and Hvergelmir the place where the souls of the most wicked were consumed by the giant serpent. If this coincidence of imagery between pagan beliefs and the saga's text were in fact intended, it may add yet more degradation to the method used for Ragnar's death since it signals that Ella finds him to be not a noble enemy but rather a dishonorable murderer. It is also possible that a link was intended to be made between Ragnar and Gunnar from the *Saga of the Volsungs*, who also meets his end in a pit of snakes.

[xcix] This is a significantly shortened version of the *Krákumál*, a 29-stave poem purported to be Ragnar's death-song. In fact, the *Krákumál* is a twelfth-century creation, probably written somewhere in the Scottish islands.

[c] Payment of wergild was an important practice in ancient Germanic and Scandinavian societies. The purpose of wergild was to compensate a victim—or the victim's family, if the victim had been killed—for the hurt they had received through the perpetrator's commission of a crime. The amount to be paid varied depending on the nature of the injury and the gender and social status of the parties concerned. Once wergild had been paid, the victim and/or their family had to relinquish any right to exact further payment or vengeance.

[ci] Some of the sources I consulted said that "Lundunaborg" was London;

others said that it was Lincoln. Neither identification can be historically accurate since both London and Lincoln were founded by the Romans long before the Vikings ever arrived in England. Peter Munch is in the "London" camp in his *Norse Mythology: Legends of Gods and Heroes* (New York: American-Scandinavian Foundation, 1926), p. 251. Katharine F. Boult, on the other hand, claims that Ivar's stronghold was Lincoln. *Asgard & the Norse Heroes* (London: J. M. Dent & Sons, Ltd., [1914]), p. 253.

[cii] The medieval sources do not agree on exactly what Ella's torture and death entailed. Some seem to indicate that the image of an eagle was carved into his back, but another version states that the "eagle" was created by cracking open the victim's rib cage from the back and then splaying his lungs out as though they were wings. Historian Anders Winroth says that the difficulty in translating the original Old Norse has led to other misunderstandings of the "blood eagle." Winroth says that the interpretation in which an eagle is carved into Ella's back with a knife likewise may be a mistranslation, although he finds it grammatically correct, and that it might have been the saga creator's original intent to say that Ella was killed and then his body left as food for birds of prey. *The Age of the Vikings* (Princeton: Princeton University Press, 2014), pp. 36-7.

[ciii] Quoted in Henry Resnick, "The Hobbit-Forming World of J. R. R. Tolkien," *The Saturday Evening Post* (2 July 1966), p. 94. Tolkien was less sanguine about the Celtic influences on his work and was offended when an early reviewer of *The Silmarillion* said they noticed a Celtic influence. Marjorie J. Burns, *Perilous Realms: Celtic and Norse in Tolkien's Middle-earth* (Toronto: University of Toronto Press, 2005), n.p., accessed via Google Books, 18 March 2020 <http://www.google.com/books>.

[civ] Humphrey Carpenter, *Tolkien: A Biography* (Boston: Houghton Mifflin Company, 1977), pp. 22, 35-36.

[cv] Carpenter, *Tolkien,* p. 34-5.

[cvi] Carpenter, *Tolkien*, p. 71.

[cvii] Carpenter, *Tolkien*, pp. 111, 200.

[cviii] J. R. R. Tolkien, "On Fairy-Stories," in *Essays Presented to Charles Williams* (London: Oxford University Press, 1947), p. 64.

[cix] Jonathan Evans, "The Dragon-Lore of Middle Earth: Tolkien and Old English and Old Norse Tradition," in *J. R. R. Tolkien and His Literary Resonances: Views of Middle Earth*, ed. George Clark and Daniel Timmons (Westport: Greenwood Press, 2000), 21-38.

[cx] Evans, "Dragon-Lore," p. 31.

[cxi] Margaret Schlauch, trans., *The Saga of the Volsungs: The Saga of Ragnar Lodbrok Together with the Lay of Kraka* (New York: The American Scandinavian Foundation, 1930), p. 96; J. R. R. Tolkien, *The Hobbit* (Boston: Houghton Mifflin Company, 1966), p. 262.

[cxii] Schlauch, *Volsungs*, p. 95; Tolkien, *Hobbit*, p. 240.

[cxiii] Tolkien, *Hobbit*, p. 261.
[cxiv] Schlauch, *Volsungs*, p. 101.
[cxv] Schlauch, *Volsungs*, pp. 96-7.
[cxvi] J. R. R. Tolkien, *The Silmarillion*, ed. Christopher Tolkien (Boston: Houghton Mifflin Company, 1977), p. 213-14
[cxvii] Tolkien, *Silmarillion*, p. 214
[cxviii] Tolkien, *Silmarillion*, p. 223.
[cxix] Tolkien, *Silmarillion*, p. 225.
[cxx] Tolkien, *Silmarillion*, p. 225.
[cxxi] Tolkien, *Hobbit*, p. 25.
[cxxii] Tolkien, *Hobbit*, p. 234.
[cxxiii] Tolkien, *Hobbit.* p. 235.
[cxxiv] Tolkien, *Hobbit*, p. 235.
[cxxv] Schlauch, *Volsungs*, p. 96-9.
[cxxvi] See, for example, Phelim O'Neill, "Vikings: Don't Dismiss This Show as Game of Thrones-Lite," *The Guardian* (23 May 2014), <https://www.theguardian.com/tv-and-radio/tvandradioblog/2014/may/23/vikings-review-history-channel-game-of-thrones>, accessed 9 Mar 2020.
[cxxvii] See, for example, George Sim Johnston, "The History Channel Gets *Vikings* Precisely Wrong," *The American Spectator* (12 March 2013), <https://spectator.org/33770_history-channel-gets-vikings-precisely-wrong/>, accessed 9 Mar 2020.
[cxxviii] Michael Hirst, "Foreword," in *The World of Vikings* by Justin Pollard (San Francisco, Chronicle Books, 2015), p. 5.
[cxxix] John Haywood, *Northmen: The Viking Saga AD 793-1241* (New York: St. Martin's Press, 2015), p. 98.
[cxxx] Haywood, *Northmen*, pp. 99-100.
[cxxxi] Johnston, "The History Channel."
[cxxxii] Johnston, "The History Channel."
[cxxxiii] Anders Winroth, *The Age of the Vikings* (Princeton: Princeton University Press, 2014), p. 143.
[cxxxiv] Winroth, *Age of the Vikings*, p. 136.
[cxxxv] Johnston, "The History Channel."
[cxxxvi] James Graham-Campbell, ed., *Cultural Atlas of the Viking World* (Oxford: Andromeda, 1994), p. 43.

Printed in Great Britain
by Amazon